Never accept the status quo!

THE FRAGILE MIND

How It Has Produced and Unwittingly
Perpetuates America's Tragic Disparities

Jarik E. Conrad, Ed.D.

Motivational PRESS
LEADERS IN GLOBAL PUBLISHING

Published by Motivational Press, Inc.
1777 Aurora Road
Melbourne, Florida, 32935
www.MotivationalPress.com

Manufactured in the United States of America.

ISBN: 978-1-62865-246-8

CONTENTS

PART I
THE AMERICAN EXPERIMENT: THE ORIGINS OF OUR DISPARITIES

PART II
PERPETUATING THE DISPARITIES: DANCING TO OUR DOOM

PART III
A NEW APPROACH TO INCLUSION

ACKNOWLEDGEMENTS

This second edition of The Fragile Mind could not be possible without the support and encouragement of my family and friends, as well as the positive responses from the many readers of the first publication. I have heard from individuals all over the country who have shared with me that the book has fundamentally changed how they see the world, which is the ultimate reward for writing this kind of book. Surprisingly, the positive feedback has come from both sides of the political isle, which is hard to accomplish these days.

I want to thank Unity First for their Salute to World Class Excellence Award. The purpose of the annual award is to recognize "role models who have taken diversity, leadership, and inclusion to the next level of success by changing communities, corporations, institutions, and in some cases the marketplace for the better." I also want to thank the Independent Publishers Book Awards for their Bronze Medal.

None of this would have been possible without the love and support of my wife, Adrienne. She has patiently listened and challenged me as I have worked through my thoughts about the pressing issues presented in this book. I am lucky to have her. It is important that I thank my mother,

Rita "Cutie," for her strength and courage; I am so fortunate to inherit that from her. I would also like to thank my little ones, Alexandria (Alex) and Jarik, Jr. (JC), for inspiring me to do my part to make the world a better place for them.

I want to acknowledge members of both of my fraternities, Kappa Alpha Psi and Sigma Pi Phi for their continued support. I also want to thank Angelica Kendrick, who works with me at The Conrad Consulting Group, LLC., for her research efforts for the book. I sincerely appreciate my friends Michael Crawford, Thomas Hadja, Susan Hamilton, and Chip Webster for their review, feedback, and editing of several drafts of this version of the book. I want to especially thank my new friend, Dr. Steven Southwick, co-author of *Resilience*, for helping me get the technical information about the brain correct. I cannot forget to thank once more the following people for reading the original manuscript and providing me with their valuable feedback: Dr. Christine Arab, Dr. Laura Baitlet, Michael Boylan, Clanzenetta "Mickee" Brown, Reykjavick Calhoun, Henry Luke, Lisa Moore, Bill Scheu, Harlan Stallings, Carlos Stanford, and Ron Townsend.

I have had the fortunate opportunity to address thousands as the keynote speaker at association, corporate, and nonprofit events. I want to thank those audience members for lending me their ears and minds for the time we spent together and offering such moving feedback. I would also like to offer a special thanks to my present and past clients for the opportunity to work with them to develop better leaders and create more inclusive organizations.

Foreword

Race is one of the most difficult subjects for Americans to talk about. The conversations rarely happen, and when they do, they generally become divisive and unproductive. The result has been disastrous. I am not an expert on this issue, but I am among the countless Americans ready for a change. Dr. Conrad represents such a change in both style and substance.

Dr. Conrad not only takes us on an extraordinary open and honest personal journey, he also builds upon these experiences with the latest research findings in psychology and neuroscience. What unfolds is an innovative approach to the age-old challenge of how people understand and deal with racial differences.

In The Fragile Mind, you will not find the political dogma, emotional rants, or superficial sound bites that are common in discussions about race. Rather, regardless or your political views or personal experiences, Dr. Conrad presents a cogent analysis that will engage and empower you.

The Fragile Mind belongs in the personal library of anyone who is frustrated with America's ongoing issues with race, but at a loss about what can be done to speed up the process of change. Dr. Conrad helps readers understand how we got to this point, and more importantly, how we can move forward to unite the country to a degree that has never been achieved.

As the CEO of Motivational Press, I chose to publish the Fragile Mind because I know it has the potential to fundamentally change the debate about race in America. As a best-selling author, I will be recommending it to all of my readers, who are continually looking for ways to improve - both personally and professionally.

Justin Sachs

Founder and CEO

Justin Sachs Companies

PREFACE

Education is the most powerful weapon

which you can use

to change the world.

—Nelson Mandela

A lot has happened regarding race relations in America since the publication of the first edition of *The Fragile Mind* in 2008. I felt it necessary to revise the book to sharpen the arguments made in the previous version, as well as to include some insight into recent developments. The most notable event has been the election of America's first Black President, Barack Obama. Individuals who thought that such a momentous feat would open the door to racial understanding and reconciliation in America have had to think again.

EXTREMIST GROUPS

The number of extremists groups has skyrocketed after the election of President Obama. According to the Southern Poverty Law Center, the number of Patriot groups, including armed militias, grew from 149 in 2008 to 1360 by 2012 (Potok, 2014). That is an increase of 813%. The number of hate groups grew from 888 in 2007 to a record high of 1,018 by 2011 (Potok, 2014). Membership in such groups, however, is starting to decline. Lone wolves or pairs of extremists who don't belong to any organization have carried out over 90% of domestic terrorist attacks in the U.S. in recent years (Potok, 2014). Unfortunately, the recent decline of group affiliation is not necessarily because people are not hating others as much, but because rather than joining groups, some extremists are relying more on the Internet to connect with others who share their views. Another reason for the decline in numbers is that, reminiscent of the pre-Civil Rights era, some mainstream politicians are embracing extremist views. It is not unusual these days to hear political speeches that could have been taken right out of the '50s and early '60s. Unfortunately, it is not all talk.

On the evening of June 17, 2015, Dylann Roof opened fire during a service at Emanuel African Methodist Episcopal Church in Charleston, South Carolina. Roof's rampage left nine dead. While some Americans questioned whether the act was motivated by racial hatred or religious hatred, Roof made his motivations clear posting among other things on social media, "We have no skinheads, no real KKK, no one doing anything but talking on the internet. Well someone has to have the bravery to take it to the real world, and I guess that has to be me" (Daily Beast, 2015). Roof's heinous act shocked the nation and drew immediate disdain from people across the country because it involved such a significant loss of life at church of all places, but Roof is not alone in his willingness to take hate "to the real world." There are approximately 191,000 reported and unreported hate crimes in America each year ("Hate incidents," n.d.). From 1995 to 2012, race was the primary reason for the majority of hate crimes ("Hate incidents," n.d.).

Moreover, Blacks were the main targets in these crimes. According to the FBI Uniform Crime Reports, hate crimes motivated by race occur at almost double the rate of all other hate crimes combined. Blacks are more than three times as likely to be victims of hate crimes than Whites (Federal Bureau of Investigation [FBI], 2013).

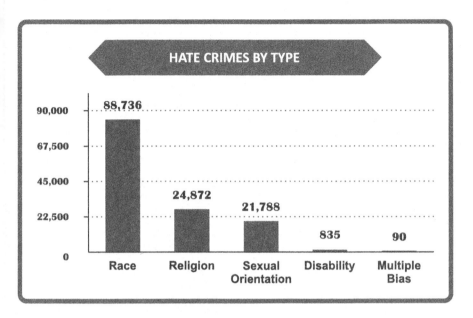

The Southern Poverty Law Center and FBI data make it clear that there are significant numbers of Whites in America who still hate Blacks, yet, inexplicably, some Whites find it absurd to believe that some of the criticism of President Obama is generated out of racial animus. On the other hand, some Blacks are over-protective and overly defensive when there is criticism of the President. It doesn't take much, though, to see how they can feel that way. Read the online comment sections of many newspapers in the country, and it becomes clear that some people are not happy about having a Black President; under the cloak of anonymity, they come right out and say it. I, for example, wrote a balanced article a few years ago for a local newspaper that asked me to explore the impact of race on people's feelings of President Obama. I only presented obvious evidence of racial bias such as hurtful racist comments and highly offensive signs that people were holding up at rallies. It seemed that few of the people who commented even bothered to read the article given the level of venom and misinformation it generated. I was called a "race baiter." People questioned how I could afford the suit I wore in the photo that appeared in the article, and several people assumed that I obtained my education only because of Affirmative Action. There were no specific comments questioning any of the facts I had presented.

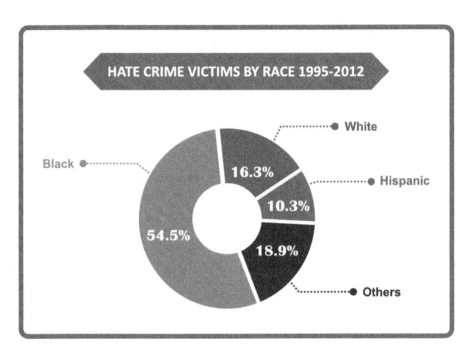

POLICE SHOOTINGS

If the next few weeks are anything like the past few weeks, there will be a shooting somewhere in America that involves a White police officer and an unarmed Black victim. It seems odd that authorities over the years have been able to successfully arrest violent criminals such as Jeffrey Dahmer, Dennis Rader (B2K), Charles Manson, and a host of other really dangerous White guys, yet unarmed Black people who stole cigars, sold loose cigarettes, had a busted tail light, or committed no crime at all have ended up shot dead by the police. Despite conclusive video evidence, the response has been individuals playing their respective race cards. Like clockwork, when the next incident happens, many Whites will believe the police officer was in fear for his or her life, so justified in pulling the trigger. Predictably, many Blacks will believe the victim was targeted and treated inhumanely. There will be varying degrees of the role of race in the altercation. White shooters and observers will inevitably deny that race was a factor in the incident. Black victims (if alive) and observers will inevitably argue that race was the primary factor in the incident.

The fact of the matter is that when there has been video, it has often not looked good for the police. Still, these incidents rarely result in any criminal charges being brought against the officers, let alone subsequent convictions. Compared to the general public, law enforcement officers accused of crimes are less likely to be convicted or incarcerated. In 2010, there were 4,861 reports of misconduct by law enforcement officers (The Cato Institute, 2010). According to The Cato Institute's National Police Misconduct Reporting Report, the conviction rate for the general public is approximately 70%, with an average length of incarceration of 49 months; the conviction rate for law enforcement officers is about 37%, with an average length of incarceration of 35 months (2010). Moreover, "if excessive force complaints involving fatalities were prosecuted as murder, the murder rate for law enforcement officers would exceed the general population murder rate by 472%" (The Cato Institute, 2010).

The reality in these unfortunate incidents is that sometimes the shooter is justified in using deadly force, and sometimes he or she is not. Sometimes race subconsciously biases the decision to pull the trigger and other times race consciously biases that decision. Each of these incidents needs to be examined individually, but looking at the overall trends helps us to ask the right questions. According to a Propublica article, "the 1,217 deadly police shootings from 2010 to 2012 captured in the federal data show that Black males, age 15 to 19, were killed at a rate of 31.17 per million, while just 1.47 per million White males in that age range died at the hands of police" (Gabrielson, Jones, & Sagara, 2014). It is no mystery why there is there a lack of trust toward police within Black communities across America.

Officer 1: "Do you celebrate quanza [sic] at your school?"

Officer 2, "Yeah we burn the cross on the field! Then we celebrate Whitemas."

Officer 1: "Cross burning lowers blood pressure! I did the test myself!"

Officer 1: "All n****rs must fucking hang,"

Officer 2 "Ask my 6 year old what he thinks about Obama."

Officer 1: "Niggers should be spayed,"

Officer 2: "I saw one an hour ago with 4 kids."

Officer 1: "We got two Blacks at my boys [sic] school and they are brother and sister! There 'cause dad works for the school district and I am watching them like hawks."

Officer 1: "'I hate to tell you this but my wife friend [sic] is over with their kids and her husband is Black! If [sic] is an Attorney but should I be worried?'"

Officer 2: "Get ur pocket gun. Keep it available in case the monkey returns to his roots. Its [sic] not against the law to put an animal down."

Officer 1: "Well said!"

Officer 1: "Its [sic] worth every penny to live here [Walnut Creek] away from the savages."

Officer 1: "White Power"

These are not transcripts from 1940s court cases. The transcripts are of text messages exchanged among fourteen White San Francisco police officers between 2011 and 2012 that became public as part of a federal corruption trial against one of the officers who had been convicted of stealing money and drugs from suspects (Shapiro, 2015; Van Derbeken, J. 2015; Williams, 2015). Retired judges are now reviewing over 3,000 cases these officers handled to assess whether bias affected the outcomes. Similarly, in Ferguson, Missouri, the Department of Justice found "a pattern or practice of unlawful conduct within the Ferguson Police Department that violates the First, Fourth, and Fourteenth Amendments to the United States Constitution and federal statutory law" (United States Department of Justice, 2015). The fact that body cameras are not issued to every officer given what we have learned from examples like San Francisco and Ferguson is astonishing. After Rialto, California, implemented body cameras, the police force experienced 88% fewer complaints than they had over the previous 12 months. Moreover, use of force by officers fell by almost 60% over the same period (Lovett, 2013). Body cameras would offer better protection for officers and citizens.

Think about Black people's distrust of law enforcement in terms of classic conditioning: "An organism that remembers a past danger can recognize a similar potential danger in the future, and respond accordingly" (Southwick, & Charney, 2012). Just imagine how the San Francisco cops who exchanged those text messages treated the Black people they would come across on the streets each day. They clearly thought of them as animals; they admitted as much in their texts. It is clear to me that the majority of cops are not bad apples. I participated in a special program conducted by the police in Jacksonville, Florida, designed to educate community leaders regarding some of the incredible challenges law enforcement personnel deal with on a regular basis. Over the course of a few weeks, we had the opportunity to observe SWAT team training, participate in a prostitution sting, observe a drug bust, visit the jail, fire weapons at the shooting range, and try out the simulator. To my wife's chagrin, a few of us even volunteered to be briefly tased. This program was helpful in understanding just how difficult a job it is to be a cop. It was obvious from my interaction with them that most of the officers were responsible people who loved their jobs. The problem is that citizens don't know who is and who isn't a bad apple, so they are cautious with all police. This is not about paranoia; it's about survival.

OTHER HIGH-PROFILE INCIDENTS REGARDING RACE

"Stand your ground" legal conflicts between Black and White citizens add to the specter of growth in extremists and questionable police shootings. When these major conflicts between Blacks and Whites occur, a common cry is, "race had nothing to do with it." I can remember watching an interview on television with a Black jurist from a high-profile case during 2012 in Jacksonville, Florida, where the defendant, Michael Dunn, was accused of shooting into a car of four teenagers after getting into an altercation over their loud music. One of the teenagers, Jordan Davis, was killed. This incident happened a few blocks from my home. The jurist indicated that race did not come up even one time during the jury's deliberations. The prosecutors did all they could to keep the discussion of race out of the courtroom. Dunn was found guilty of three counts of second-degree attempted murder, but the trial ended in a mistrial on the murder charge. Although Dunn was eventually convicted of first-degree murder in a second trial, it was concerning that his feelings towards race were not raised during either trial given that the letters he wrote from jail while awaiting trial made several references to race. Referring to North Florida, Dunn wrote, "They seem to have a lot of racial guilt, or at least the prosecutor's office does" (WOKV, 2013). He also commented, "This jail is full of blacks and they all act like thugs" (WOKV, 2013). I am not in Dunn's head, and I was not there when he pulled the trigger, so I can't say with certainty that race was the motivating factor in the altercation, but the possibility should have at least been explored. Dunn, like George Zimmerman in the Travon Martin case, said he was afraid for his life. In both cases, not only did these men initiate the altercation, but also they were the only ones armed.

It is commonly believed that Americans don't talk enough about race. I believe we talk about it a lot, just not intelligently. Even when people such as celebrity chef Paula Deen, actor Michael Richards from *Seinfeld*, wrestling legend Hulk Hogan, reality television star Duane "Dog" Chapman, former L.A. Clippers owner Donald Sterling, or members of the University of Oklahoma chapter of Sigma Alpha Epsilon make obviously racist comments, you can count on them to acknowledge that they made a mistake while quickly asserting that they are not racist. The cop who was the most prolific texter in the San Francisco Police Department investigation even claims that he is not racist. Each one of these folks can offer examples of Black people with whom they are close friends as proof that they could not be racist. For instance, not only did Sterling have a Black coach and team full of Black players who helped generate great wealth for him, but his mistress to whom he made his racist comments was also mixed race.

Summary

Americans need a better approach to race relations. In none of the dialogue about race have I heard discussion about what I call the neuroscience of race. Concepts that will be explored in this book such as mirror neurons, inattention blindness, complex trauma, vicarious traumatization, sense of foreshortened future, and persistent traumatic stress all play a role in creating perceptions and outcomes regarding race in America. Instead, what I hear are debates between people with narrow viewpoints filled with guilt, anger, frustration, sadness, and hopelessness. While those emotions are real, they are often misplaced and do not move us closer to solutions. It is senseless for Blacks to be angry at Whites today for something that happened in the 1800s, and it's pointless for Whites to feel guilty about what their great-great-grandfathers did. However, it is every citizen's responsibility to understand the legacy of the country's past atrocities, as well as what factors perpetuate the hardships that Blacks continue to experience. One of the reasons viewpoints are so narrow is the fact that the country is still very segregated. Partly because of discriminatory housing policies that I will address later in this book, there are still many people in this country who have no significant relationship with anyone from a different racial background. Over 86% of Whites live in neighborhoods where minorities make up less than 1 percent of the population. In the U.S., 80% of Whites live outside of cities while 70% of Blacks and Latinos live in the cities or inner-ring suburbs. ("Go deeper: Where race lives," n.d.).

Talking about race is one thing; experiencing racial differences in one's daily life is another. The widespread segregation affects how Blacks and Whites see themselves and each other. I believe tensions across racial lines, such as that between police and Black communities, will subside only with relationship building. *The Fragile Mind* offers an approach to help build such relationships. The approach, which is based on innovative applications of the most recent developments in neuroscience, represents the best chance for Americans to finally conquer its race problem and reach new levels of prominence.

INTRODUCTION

A TANGLED WEB: THE STATE OF RACE RELATIONS IN AMERICA.

This year, America celebrated the 50th anniversary of the most significant piece of Civil Rights legislation in its history, the Voting Rights Act of 1965, which prohibits racial discrimination in voting. In 2013, the Supreme Court, in *Shelby County v. Holder*, handed down a controversial decision regarding a key provision of the law. Section 5 of the law prohibits covered states from making changes to their election practices and procedures without obtaining the approval of the Attorney General or the United States District Court for the District of Columbia. States that were covered under this provision had a history of enacting changes that had a discriminatory purpose or effect, such as literacy tests and poll taxes. Section 5 still stands, but the coverage formula in Section 4(b) that gave it its teeth was declared unconstitutional. In the majority opinion, Justice John Roberts cited that the formula was "based on 40-year-old facts having no logical relationship to the present day." (Shelby County

v. Holder, 2013). In other words, the country has changed so much regarding the status of Blacks that these formulas, which were last updated in 1975, were outdated.

In the years after the historic turnout of Blacks who voted Democrat during the 2008 presidential election, Republican legislatures sponsored and passed new voter ID laws in sixteen states, even though these laws have consistently been shown to adversely affect Blacks. Of the sixteen, fifteen were established after the Supreme Court Shelby County decision. Six of the sixteen states have a documented history of discriminating against Black voters. These new laws were introduced, according to their sponsors, to combat voter fraud, which was described as being rampant throughout the country. However, of the mere twenty-eight convictions for voter fraud since 2000, voter impersonation at the polls, which is what voter ID requirement aims to prevent, was evident in only one of those cases - just one. In other words, there is no statistical justification to introduce new ID requirements. On the other hand, election experts suggest the real area for concern is mail-in ballots, where 75% of the voters are White (Childress, 2014). If fraud were the major concern, it would seem that something would have been proposed to address this risk as well.

Predictably, many Whites react to voter ID laws with support. After all, having an ID seems like a reasonable requirement to protect the sanctity of the vote. Many Blacks, however, react with great concern given that these new requirements are eerily reminiscent of the tactics that were used to deny Blacks access to the polls after Reconstruction (*Section 5 of the Voting Rights Act, n.d.*). For example, in Texas, a Black grandmother who had consistently voted all her life could not afford $25 to pay for a copy of her birth certificate so that she could obtain one of the accepted forms of identification required by the new law. The $25 essentially amounts to a poll tax, which was a common penalty for being Black and wanting to vote in the South after Reconstruction. I will address in this book the larger question of why someone in her position may not be able to afford the $25, but the fact that someone who had faithfully voted for decades could not exercise her civic right because of a requirement that was suddenly put in place to overcome a perceived, but nonexistent problem is quite troubling. Thankfully, the courts have struck down some of these laws, but this is a story that will continue to unfold.

Voting rights and other legal issues serve as the perfect representation of where today's America is regarding issues related to race. Start with the fact that the Supreme Court is split along ideological lines with conservatives, who were appointed by Republicans, outnumbering liberals, who were appointed by Democrats, five to four. The Justices vote according to their ideology, so issues such as the voter ID laws garner decisions favored by conservatives. Ironically, one of the most conservative and most critical justices regarding government programs aimed at redressing historic and current discrimination against Blacks is Judge Clarence Thomas, a Black man. When he speaks out regarding these issues, it is almost as though there is more weight given to his opinions than the other Justices because, after all, he is Black, so nobody can claim racism as a factor in his harsh criticisms of these programs. Finally, add the fact that other Justices also feel that Blacks have made so much progress over the past fifty years that programs to level the playing field are no longer relevant.

Blacks have made some progress as a group, but the greatest gains have been made on an individual level. Extraordinary successes by some, such as President Obama, entrepreneurs, CEOs, etc., mask the fact that in almost every aspect of quality life, the numbers indicate that masses of Blacks are still struggling in America. Experts in economics, education, psychology, sociology, and just about every other "ology" have dissected race and poverty and the intersection of the two have had only marginal success fixing the problem. Many Whites get angry when racism is mentioned as a significant factor in the socioeconomic status of Blacks and immediately accuse Blacks of playing the race card. The interesting thing about the race card is that it is perceived by Whites to have so much influence, yet if it were really such a powerful weapon, it is doubtful that

Blacks would continue to struggle to such a significant degree. Moreover, Whites fail to see that when they blindly jump to the defense of other Whites, they are themselves playing the race card.

So what is really going on? There can only be four possible explanations for the struggles of Blacks in America: (1) Black people are simply genetically inferior; (2) something is happening to them that makes it very difficult for them to succeed, (3) they are doing something that makes it difficult for them to succeed; or (4) a combination of these factors is occurring. Despite recurring efforts in American history to prove otherwise, such as the eugenics movement, there exists no scientific evidence to suggest that Blacks, or any other racial group for that matter, are genetically inferior or superior. There is not even a biological basis for the term "race" - it is a socially created construct. Reasons 1 must then be rejected. Therefore, we must explore reasons 2 and 3, that there are external forces outside of their control that are contributing to the widespread disparities that Blacks experience or Black people are making poor decisions and engaging in self-destructive behaviors. I believe what's happening is a combination of these two factors.

My approach in this book rejects the misguided "either/or" notion in popular discourse that claims either outright discrimination by Whites or simply a lack of personal responsibility by Blacks is the cause of the sobering disparities. We are all complicit in this problem, and the culprit is our vulnerable minds. As brilliant as the human mind is, its design sometimes works against us. The mind's fragility has resulted in individual, institutional, and structural bias by some Whites in America, as well as complacency and irresponsibility by some Blacks. In the three sections of this book, I will explore the factors that explain (1) how we got to this point in the first place; (2) why we continue to struggle; and (3) how we can move forward. As you read this book, I ask that you avoid jumping to convenient, emotion-driven conclusions. I want to challenge you to think beyond sound bites, unqualified opinions, and biased reporting. Discovering the answers to the challenges that inhibit the ability for all

Americans to work, live, and play together will require each of us to think deeply, perhaps more deeply than we have at any point in our lives.

There are a handful of typical reactions to some of the harsh realities that I address in this book. First, people just don't believe, or claim they don't believe the facts. For them, all I can do is cite references. Second, people point out that it's not patriotic to criticize your country. I want to help them understand that blind patriotism is a dangerous thing. There are people all over committing unspeakable acts of terror in the name of patriotism. On a practical level, one can love his or her family deeply, but still acknowledge some familial flaws. Third, some people suggest that if Blacks are so unhappy, they should go elsewhere. People who feel this way need to be reminded that there is no racial claim to America. The first immigrants to arrive in America had no such concept as race. Further, it is well documented that Blacks and other peoples of color provided the free and discounted labor to build this country. Only the Native Americans can argue that this is their country because they were never immigrants. A fourth common reaction is that there are worse places than America to live. It is true that even with its warts, people are literally killing themselves trying to get to America to escape worse situations in their countries. Rather than comparing America to those countries, I hope we would hold America to a different standard. Let's work hard to really be who we claim to be—a place where opportunities exist for all based on performance. Finally, there are those who promote patience; they feel that things keep getting better with time (Pew Research Center, 2010). However, while the polls suggest that they may be more likely to have friends or even marry nonwhites, research shows that White millennials have not demonstrated a deep understanding of the complex issues surrounding race and poverty nor the desire to enact programs to close racial gaps. Regarding support for various government programs aimed at eliminating racial inequity, 17-34 year-old Whites have more in common with older Whites (65+) than they do with Blacks in the same age group. Blacks are four times more likely to support any type of government aid to Blacks or affirmative action programs for schools or employers. Other research examining a battery of questions designed to measure egalitarianism found that younger Whites had the same level of racial stereotypes as their parents (McElwee, 2015).

SUMMARY

The disparities in America persist not because Whites are superior or because Blacks are inferior, but rather because we all are human. As such, we can all be victims of subtle vulnerabilities that shape our perspective and resulting behavior. Looking at ourselves in the mirror and acknowledging our flaws doesn't make us weak; it makes us strong. Think of *The Fragile Mind* as a mirror into which we can peer to get the honest feedback we need to move forward and become the greatest nation we can be.

I am not a neuroscientist, psychiatrist, or psychologist. I hope this book can be an invitation to get more of these experts in the discussion of race in America. I know that have only scratched the surface of the immense intellectual horsepower America's scientific population could bring to bear. This is not a textbook or a clinical publication. Yet, it is not a memoir, either. This is not a political book, so it is not written for conservatives and it's not written for liberals. After all, it was the Republicans in early America who initially demonstrated more empathy for Blacks; that sentiment later shifted to the Democrats, but neither party has gone all-in on really understanding the problem and finding long-term solutions. This book represents my attempt to blend science and practice in a meaningful way for decision makers—elected officials, business leaders, policymakers, educators, parents, and nonprofit leaders—to use right away to make better decisions regarding people from the different backgrounds they serve. I have endeavored to present a balanced case, but I recognize that my background and experiences have shaped who I am and how I think. After all, I have my own fragile mind with which to deal.

PART I

THE AMERICAN EXPERIMENT: THE ORIGINS OF OUR DISPARITIES

Chapter 1

Endangered Species: Growing Up Black (and Poor) in America

Poverty is like punishment for a crime you didn't commit.
And one never really forgets either—
everything serves as a constant reminder of it.

—Eli Khamarov

Growing up in East St. Louis was tough; growing up in public housing in East St. Louis was even tougher. On one hand, there are certain aspects of growing up there that I loved, and some of the smartest and kindest people I have ever met are from East St. Louis. I would not be who I am if it were not for my experiences there. On the other hand, I couldn't raise my kids there. I am deeply saddened that so many young Black kids won't have the option of growing up anywhere else.

As I travel the country as a keynote speaker addressing topics such as leadership, poverty, cultural competency, emotional intelligence (EI), and resilience, I share my experiences growing up in East St. Louis. I don't do so to cast a negative shadow over the city and its residents, but rather to shed light on the challenges so many people face in poverty-stricken pockets of America, the wealthiest country in the world. I write and speak out about these issues because I want things to change for all the young people who will be born in these places. In this chapter, I provide my firsthand account of what it is like for a young Black male trying to figure out what life is all about in a place that has been forsaken by so many.

I was in East St. Louis in 2007 for a funeral while I was working on the first edition of *The Fragile Mind*. To give readers a glimpse into what the city looked like at the time, I took the following photos of populated neighborhoods in the city. These images are not the immediate result of an earthquake, tornado, or other national disaster. These are images the residents have come to know as "normal" in their city.

My childhood home in East St. Louis.

Our garage.

Imagine what it must feel like to be a young person growing up surrounded by these images. For many, they serve as a constant reminder that the world you know is far different from the world on television. Not only does the city look like a war zone, it feels like one many of its citizens. The crime rates are alarming ("East St. Louis, Illinois," n.d.; "Crime in the United States in 2012," n.d.). In 2012, 2013, and 2014, East St. Louis was the most dangerous city in the United States, according to research done by neighborhoodscout.com (Sylte, 2014). Again, imagine how you might feel knowing your city tops the charts as one of the worst places to live in the country. Moreover, imagine what that thought must do to a parent who feels responsible for helping their kids stay safe and become successful.

According to Jonathan Kozol, who writes about the poorest communities in the country, the St. Louis Post Dispatch described East

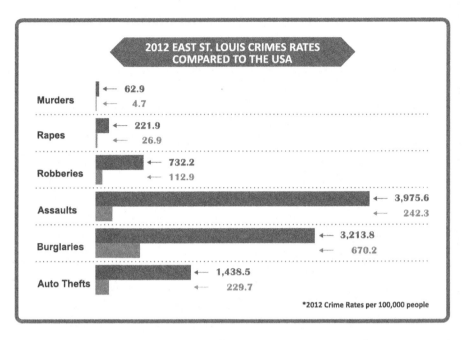

St. Louis as America's Soweto. The U.S. Department of Housing and Urban Development called East St. Louis "the most distressed small city in America" (1991). In his *New York Times* best seller *Savage Inequalities*, Kozol provides one of the best accounts of how challenging things were for residents of the city. He researched his book when I was there as a high school student from 1987 to 1990. Then, nearly a third of East St. Louis families lived on less than $7,500 a year, and 75% of its population lived on welfare of some form (Kozol, 1991). Not much has changed; the median household income in East St. Louis is now $17,756, compared to $55,137 for the state. The unemployment rate is 17%; the high school graduation rate is 73% compared to a state average of 86%; and only 9.2 percent of its residents have a bachelor's degree or higher ("East St. Louis, Illinois," n.d). Moreover, only 5 percent of its graduates are "ready for college coursework" (Illinois Report Card 2013-2014, n.d.).

The chair of the state board of education at the time described East St. Louis as the worst possible place he could imagine to have a child brought up (Kozol, 1991). The science lab had no equipment, the classrooms had limited supplies, and the restrooms had few working toilets. I trained myself not to have to use the restroom during school hours. If I absolutely had to have a bowel movement, I would go home. There were no swimming pools, no maintained tennis or basketball courts, no soccer fields, and no football fields or baseball diamonds at the schools. We had no cafeteria in our elementary school, so we ate our lunches at our desks. It was not unusual to have a class with twenty-six books for over 100 students, so we had to leave the books at school. Due to budget cuts during the time I was in high school, the school system fired dozens of certified teachers and replaced them with over seventy untrained "permanent substitute teachers," who were only paid $10,000 a year. The qualified teachers who survived earned a little over half of what they could have made at suburban schools (Kozol, 1991). It is amusing to me that people who warn about "not throwing money at problems" rarely suffer from a lack of resources themselves. Given these challenges, there should be no surprise that less than 55% of students regularly graduated high school back then, only 25% of those graduates went on to college, and a smaller fraction of that group earned college degrees (Kozol, 1991). On one of his research visits to the city, Dr. Kozol was approached by a young schoolgirl who asked him, "Are we citizens of East St. Louis, or are we citizens of America?" (1991).

Despite its dire conditions, East St. Louis is a place that has produced remarkable talent. Jazz great Miles Davis, Olympic superstar Jackie Joyner-Kersee, renown sociologist Harry Edwards, former U.S. ambassador and permanent representative to the United Nations Donald McHenry, legendary entertainer Katherine Dunham, and a host of professional athletes, poets, writers, doctors, lawyers, scholars, and musicians hail from East St. Louis. When I was in high school, our jazz band was recognized as the best in the nation and was frequently invited to play in Europe and Asia. My high school basketball team won three state championships in a row, despite having a flooded gym that required them to play their home games on the road one year. The girls track team at my high school won the state title fourteen out of sixteen years. The football team at our rival high school, East St. Louis Senior High, has won six state championships in football, despite most of that time having a practice field without goalposts. Some people use these accomplishments to downplay the importance of adequate resources. I can only imagine what these individuals and teams might have accomplished with more resources.

Conditions in the city were certainly demoralizing but, unlike some of my peers, I do not recall consciously feeling inferior as a young child. I knew, however, from television reports and newspaper accounts that the outside world thought of me as such. I absolutely hated that. In my desire to prove to everyone that I was not going to be just another Black male statistic on the nightly news, I developed a confidence—some might have described it as arrogance—that could not be shaken. In retrospect, maybe I was trying to prove something to myself as well as those people who counted me out at the start. Whatever the reason, I developed a belief that my family was better off than all the other families around us, so, by extension, I was somehow better and more deserving of success than all the other kids. In reality, my mother was a twice-divorced single parent on welfare. We rarely had reliable transportation. We lacked common amenities such as central air or cable television. My brother worked odd jobs and my sisters worked retail, janitorial, or fast food jobs. We did not go to white linen restaurants and rarely had money for entertainment such as going to see a movie. We used substitutes such as orange "drink" instead of more expensive orange juice. We did not go on vacation. I never owned a pair of Air Jordan's. Our diets primarily consisted of processed foods that were high in sugar, salt, and fat. I could go on, but I am sure you get the point. We were struggling!

I still, somehow, felt that we were different from my neighbors, and in some ways, we really were. There were no drugs around the house—at least that I could see. I found out later that my mother put my father out of the house and divorced him when I was five years old because she found out he had a drug addiction. None of my immediate family spent any time in jail. None of my siblings had any children while in their teens. We looked different, too. We had light skin. While not as consequential as on southern plantations in the 1800s, the light-skin/dark-skin issue was real in East St. Louis in the 1970s and 1980s. Light-skinned folks were perceived as being more intelligent and more attractive than dark-skinned people. Chandra (a.k.a. Tesha), my middle sister who is now deceased, won the first Miss East St. Louis contest in 1979. I am sure it helped that she had light skin. The skin color issue is a prime example of how fragile the human mind can be. Internalized oppression compelled some Black people to despise dark skin and admire light skin. This issue has not completely gone away today, and it is not unique to Blacks. There are ethnic groups in places such as India, the Middle East, and the Caribbean that continue to struggle with this.

Grown Too Soon?

I suppose I knew deep down at some level that we were in the same boat as everybody else, but I refused to consciously accept it. My reluctance to accept my station in life proved to be challenging for my mother. I stood with her in government "free-cheese lines," but I would not eat the cheese. I got most of my toys, books, and sports equipment as hand-me-downs from thrift stores, but I refused to wear any of the used clothes. I would not stand with her at the cash register when she would buy items with food stamps, even though my friends' parents also used food stamps. I hated using public transportation. I refused to wear the free "Coke bottle" glasses that just shouted welfare that I got from the eye doctor. I would hold them up to my eyes to see the chalkboard in school, but I would not put them on my face. I had a particular disdain for government agency offices. I hated how they treated those who came in for their help. When I would be stuck sitting in one of those offices for hours with my mother, all I could think about was growing up and doing everything in my power to ensure I would never have to sit in those places again.

Given what I have shared thus far, you might think that I would be ashamed of my mother for our family being in the situation we were in, but I was not. I was somehow convinced that our situation was a result of external forces, while everyone else was responsible for their own undoing. What bothered me most was that so many people seemed to be okay with struggling; they seemed to revel in being the underdog—a theme that would later play out in so many hip-hop lyrics. What I realize now is that this sense of pride was merely masking a debilitating fear and sense of hopelessness. So many people in that community had asked themselves on a conscious or subconscious level, "why try?" They were paralyzed by fear of failure. They had developed a learned helplessness, as described in the 1967 study where dogs failed to escape shock when they had the opportunity to do so after they had experienced repeated inescapable shocks (Overmier & Seligman, 1967).

Somehow I never accepted the presupposition that I should settle for less because I was Black and born in the ghetto. I refused to be weighed down by any invisible chains. Despite her being somewhat frustrated, my mother recognized this in me and started to feed this behavior. She often told me that I was different, better than everyone else in the neighborhood. She treated me differently than the other parents, or single parent, treated their kids. She took me everywhere with her, whether kids were allowed or not. I spent most of my childhood sitting at kitchen tables with older adults gambling and playing cards before my feet could even touch the ground. The time I spent with adults was evident in my language. I cursed and used foul language almost as soon as I learned to talk, something that was not unusual in my family. Some of my niece Chandria's first words, for instance, were "dat-dam" when she dropped her bottle or pacifier. I was a little bolder. I had long hair as a preschooler, so people would often mistake me for a girl. When someone would comment how pretty of a girl I was, I pulled down my pants and yelled to them, "I ain't no gotdam girl … see!" I was never really disciplined for cursing because everybody thought it was cute. I could not imagine raising my kids this way now, but kids grow up fast in the alternate reality that is America's ghettoes.

Hanging out with adults led to some interesting interactions. Slim, a man who lived a couple of doors down from us in the Villa Griffin projects, knocked on our door one evening. My mother asked him how he was doing and wanted to know what she could do for him. Slim asked, "Is Jarik here?" I must have been eight or nine years old at the time. My mother looked at him strangely and called me downstairs. Slim asked if he could borrow some money from me until he got his check. It must have been about $20 or something. Everybody knew I carried a wallet but hated to spend my own money on anything. I did well in those card games, too, so I had plenty of money. I agreed to lend him the money, but only if he gave me more back. I am sure that I had never heard of interest at that point in my life, but it just made sense to me that I should get something extra out of the deal. Slim and I did a lot of business together in those days. Looking back on it, Slim had probably been squandering his money on drugs or alcohol, and I was likely enabling his addiction.

I cringe as I write this, but I can remember that, as an elementary school student, my mother left the decision to me about whether to go to school on any given day. To her defense, she knew how much I enjoyed school and that I would never miss anything important. While this was certainly a risky approach, I took the responsibility seriously. I liked the fact that I could make decisions that other kids were not allowed to make. I even stopped cursing in elementary school when I learned other kids were just learning curse words. I guess I was like, "Been there, done that." While this would not work for most kids, the high level of trust my mother placed in me helped to shape my expectations of myself and of those around me. This was just another reminder to me that I was different.

Cultural Diversity?

The overwhelming majority of the residents, 97%, of East St. Louis were Black. The only White classmates I can recall in school were Mike in elementary and a wannabe gangster who transferred into my junior high. Predictably, he didn't last very long. The only White adults I had a significant amount of interaction with growing up were Mr. Willgas, Mr. Bedwell, Mr. Lindsey and Jim, our mail carrier. Mr. Michael Willgus was the elementary school's gifted program teacher. We did not have a gifted program housed at each school, so high-achieving kids from each of the city's elementary schools were bussed one day each week to a separate school to take gifted classes. Mr. Bedwell was one of our high school guidance counselors. His style was unconventional, and his language was not PG, but it was evident that he cared about the students. Mr. Lindsey, the high school physics teacher, was terrorized by the students each day. His class was like a television sitcom. Students did everything from cursing him out, to hiding his materials, to toying with his toupee or trying to glue his glasses to his face. I don't know how he survived. When we lived in the projects, Jim, the mail carrier, frequently stopped by our unit instead of our neighbors' to eat his lunch, only adding to our feeling of superiority.

The only Asians I interacted with growing up were the Koreans who owned the beauty supply stores and the Chinese who owned the takeout restaurants. It always troubled me that the beauty supply store owners made so much money selling products to Blacks that they did not even use themselves, such as Black hair care products, hair weave, and acrylic fingernails. I never saw them reinvest that money into the community in any way other than to buy additional stores. They didn't hire Black workers or serve on the school board or civic organizations. They didn't buy homes in the city or even appear to shop at local stores. Not much has changed in poor Black communities across the United States. There are over 9,000 Asian-owned beauty supply stores serving a billion dollar market for Black hair (Asmerom, 2010).

I didn't know so at the time, but the Chinese "rice-houses" in East St. Louis are quite unique. The experience is very impersonal and somewhat offensive. Customers place their order through a bulletproof glass partition resembling a ticket window at a stadium. The food is slid to the customer through a drive-thru type of drawer. These places are strictly carryout, often having only one table if that in their small, graffiti-riddled waiting areas. When we were kids, it seemed as though the more dangerous the place was, the better the food. Two gunmen robbed my friend Vic and his cousin at one of these places and probably would have shot them had they not fought them off. My sister, Ladybug, had her purse snatched at another rice-house despite tussling with her assailant. My friends and I developed a system where a couple of people would go into the rice house and get the food while others stayed outside on guard, but it was still a risky proposition. You might wonder why people would go to such dangerous places. One major reason is that here were also limited food options in the city, particular ones that stayed open late at night. We had no upscale restaurants and few chain establishments. Delivery services did not run in East St. Louis for fear that the drivers would be robbed. It was not just restaurants that were the problem. Researchers have referred to places like East St. Louis as "food deserts" because of the lack of available, affordable, nutritious foods (Cummins & Macintyre, 2002). Most people shopped at expensive convenience stores because of the lack of nearby full-service grocery stores. It's no coincidence that people in these types of communities are more likely overweight and unhealthy.

DEAR MOMMA

Our experience with Jim provides a glimpse of my mother's contradictory views toward Whites—a love/hate relationship. On one hand, I have sensed a subtle and often not so subtle anger toward them from her over the years. She has frequently referred to Whites as "those people," "they," or "them." On the other hand, I have seen her admiration of White people. She seems proud to be fair skinned and enjoys when people mistake her for being something other than "regular" Black. To this day, she tells anybody who asks, "I ain't no African." Her father was of mixed race, and she seems proud that she has White relatives not too far down the line. She often tells stories about people treating her differently during her childhood because she looked White. I describe her behavior as that of hating the club until they invite you to become a member. It seems that to her, Jim's eating with us, or people mistaking her for something other than Black, put her one step closer to membership.

When I think about my mother's complex relationship with Whites from the perspective of the human mind's fragility, I can better understand her struggle; it is the same struggle that plagues many of her generation. Imagine living the last eighty years as a Black woman in America. There were things she could not do, places she could not go, water fountains and bathrooms she could not use, and jobs that she could not hold just because she was Black. She has witnessed and been the victim of subtle and overt acts of racism all her life. It is interesting that some Whites can't understand how people like my mother could be cautious of or even angry at Whites, but just imagine how angry they get at the mere notion that someone may have mistreated them. One can even get called a racist today for pointing out racist acts by Whites.

For some Blacks of my mother's generation, anger, resentment, and disdain seem to be the prominent feelings directed at Whites. However, considering that most of the authority figures in my mother's early life, such as school teachers and administrators, law enforcement personnel, business owners, doctors, and hiring officers, were White, it would be difficult for any young Black person to grow up in that environment without at least subconsciously buying into the idea that Whites were better than Blacks. If all the messages you receive suggest that you do not stack up, you would have to be very special to resist believing these messages. Conversely, it is not difficult to imagine what a young White person might have thought about Blacks and about themselves growing up in such an environment. If all the messages you receive suggest that you are better than others simply based on race, you would have to be very strong to resist believing that at some level you really are better than others. Believing the rhetoric about their superiority does not make Whites of that generation evil—it makes them human. Believing the rhetoric about their inferiority does not make Blacks of that generation evil—it makes them human.

MY CREATIVE OUTLET

There were many early influences in my life from which I benefited. Though I loved school and was always a good student, some of the experiences that mattered most occurred outside of the classroom. One of those early experiences was the theater. My mother began taking college courses at Southern Illinois University at Edwardsville (SIUE) when I was about nine or ten years old. Because she took me everywhere, the times that I was not in my own classes, I was in her classes. I really enjoyed attending class with her and I wanted so badly to participate in the discussions. I would get my chance with the school's Unity Theatre Ensemble. The group presented productions to colleges, universities, and civic events throughout the United States, as well as provided theater arts training to SIUE students and the community. My mother decided to join the group and, of course, I went with her to rehearsals each night. One evening, one of the cast members was sick and unable to be there. Ralph Greene, the director, asked me to stand-in for the absent cast member and read the script so that the rest of the group could understand where they were supposed to be. He reached to hand me the script, but I informed him that I didn't need it. "What do you mean you don't need it?" he asked. "Well, I have been coming to these rehearsals every night, so I know the whole script," I said unassumingly. As you might imagine, he was skeptical, so he asked me to recite a few lines. As I began reciting the lines, his eyes lit up and all the other actors stopped to pay attention to me. The rest, as they say, is history. I became the youngest and one of the most popular members of the cast for the next several years.

More than just the thrill of performing, I was drawn to the types of productions we did. We performed plays about the Black experience in America. We performed poetry by greats, such as James Baldwin, Sterling Brown, Paul Laurence Dunbar, and Langston Hughes. The experience with this material had a tremendous effect on me. It was a connection for me to sad but very important eras in American history, such as slavery. Many of us—Black and White—try to block this long, ugly chapter in the nation's history out of our consciousness. I experienced a connection to my ancestors through their words at such a young age, so I make a deliberate effort not to ignore that period. I can remember lying in bed late at night learning my lines and wondering how my life might have been different had I been born into slavery. I still think about it today. What kind of slave would I have been? Rebellious? Docile? My complexion probably puts me in the mastah's house. Would that have been better or worse than being out in the fields? While I can only imagine what life might have been like for me, through the poignant words of those talented artists I got a glimpse into the extraordinary courage, foresight, and determination necessary for survival under such conditions. I came to understand the pride and responsibility that came with being Black in America from words that vividly described the hardships my people had faced.

Not only did the theater experience offer me a connection to my past, but it also improved my confidence, boosted my communication skills, and enhanced my ability to read and adjust to people. I felt that if I could start from a voluminous script that I knew nothing about and end up able to convincingly occupy a character, I could accomplish almost anything. It's a crime that not every kid gets an opportunity to explore a creative outlet.

ONE OF POVERTY'S DAILY CHALLENGES: UNRELIABLE TRANSPORTATION

While my confidence in my abilities was strong, daily challenges would certainly test my optimism. Many of these challenges involved unreliable transportation. Once my friend Harlan and I were riding home on the expressway in one of my raggedy cars when rain started pelting down like hail. I turned on the wipers just to learn that they did not work. It is a good thing that we both have long arms, because we had to lean forward and stick them out of the windows and use them like wipers to clear a little of the windshield as we crawled down the highway. There was also the car my family had that we used to describe as the "Flintstone" car because of a large hole in the floor. I cannot forget about the old, yellow, recycled police car my mother drove for a while. No air, no heat, and no horn was typical—and forget about a radio. One of the most memorable car stories I have is funny now, but was frightening when it happened.

I was a member of a high school fraternity called the Scholarly Lincolnites Serving Throughout the Area Sufficiently (SLICKSTAS). The group was composed of about 20 of the highest academically ranked males in the school. We mostly had fun at school events, but we managed to sneak in a community service activity or two. We all decided one Saturday night during our senior year that we would go over to St. Louis for a high school party at a hotel. About half the group had cars, or access to cars, but they were all raggedy and never worked at the same time. Vic, Harlan, and I decided to ride together in Vic's yellow Pinto station wagon. As we headed to the party, I teased Vic about how shabby his car was. My exact words were, "Sounds like the bottom is going to drop out of this damn thing." Well, the bottom did drop out. Almost as soon as I got the words out of my mouth, the drive shaft fell out. We were on the Martin Luther King, Jr. Bridge, which connects East St. Louis, Illinois, to St. Louis, Missouri over the murky Mississippi River. There were no shoulder lanes in that section of the bridge and nowhere for us to walk. As cars buzzed by, barely seeing us in enough time to avoid hitting us, we didn't know whether to sit in the car and risk getting pushed over the bridge or walk across the bridge and risk being run over. Something curious happened. Two elderly White ladies decided to stop and help us. In their brand new Cadillac, they pushed our car across the bridge and out of harm's way. Can you imagine how surprised we were that they were courageous enough to help three young Black males outside one of the most dangerous cities in America? We were certainly grateful for those women. I will never forget that several Black folks zoomed right past us on the bridge that day. The experience with those women would be the first of many such experiences where Whites have gone out of their way to help or connect with me.

Once over the bridge, you would think we would call for help and go home, right? Wrong. As if the night had not provided us with enough excitement, we decided to walk the few blocks to the hotel for the party, which turned out to be a bad move. We had our SLICKSTAS jackets on, and they generated much attention from the girls at the party, which was our intent, but we also drew the kind of attention that none of us wanted. As we prepared to leave the building after the party we heard, "Hey SLICKSTAS, bring y'alls' asses out here. We got something for y'all." We looked around and noticed people brandishing guns. They threatened to shoot us for daring to come over to St. Louis. One of our guys, a big guy who had a reputation for being tough, went over to try to negotiate, but spun back around after being struck in the head with the butt of a gun. The hotel security sensed trouble and demanded that we leave their property. We spent thirty minutes pleading with the hotel employees to call the police, but they did not want to get involved. The manager called the police only after we refused to leave. When the police arrived, I knew we had avoided something big when I heard one of the officers call one of the would-be assailants by name. To say that it was embarrassing to be escorted to our cars by the police would be an understatement, but I would rather be safe and embarrassed than proud and shot.

During my senior year in high school there was another embarrassing incident involving a raggedy car. I had a job at a clothing store in the mall. The best part about the job was being able to meet girls, which is about all a high school boy thinks about. The mall was about twenty minutes from my house in Fairview Heights, IL. One day on the way to work, my little blue Ford Escort, which my sister had passed down to me, started smoking. This was nothing unusual, but the 100-degree heat really got to the car that day because the smoke was also coming inside the car through the vents. The chemical smell nearly choked me, and the smoke fumes soaked into the fabric of my clothes. I had to pull over on the side of the highway because I could not see anything except for the thick cloud of smoke in the car. I was still about ten minutes from work and I happened to be on a stretch of road where there were no nearby exits or roadside phones to call for help. I did what any self-respecting teenager would do. I reclined my seat and hid. I made sure that the seat was back far enough so that nobody passing by could see me. Moments before the real panic set in, the smoke began to settle down. I turned the key in a last-minute attempt to avoid the humiliation of walking. The car started and I made it to work that night. Trust me, it is hard trying to impress girls when you smell like radiator fumes.

The car challenges are just some experiences that shaped who I was at the time and how I saw the world. Another vivid memory is when Vic came to my house to visit one day when we were high school seniors. It must have been another 100-degree day with a heat index of something like 110. I had a fan, but it was blowing hot air, so I turned it around in the window to see if it would pull out some of the hot air as had been our custom. It did not help. When Vic walked into my room, I was lying on the bed in my underwear dripping with sweat. He said he had never seen me looking so miserable—and so serious. I was so hot and uncomfortable that it pained me to move. I can distinctly remember telling him that I could not wait until high school was over so I could get the hell out of that place. On hot days like those, we had to microwave our food because it was too hot to turn on the oven or stand at the stove to cook. I swore that I would never live like that once I left East St. Louis. Vic and I laugh about that day now, but it was anything but funny at the time. Experiences like this fueled me to do everything I could to escape poverty.

MY UNDERGRADUATE SCHOOL EXPERIENCE

Early Struggles

I know some people say that they did not realize that they were poor growing up. That was not the case for me. Poverty was an everyday intruder in my life. I was constantly reminded about things I couldn't afford to do, things I couldn't have, and places I couldn't afford to go.

Yet, I did not have a full appreciation of just how different life was for me until I went to college. I was one of the relatively few kids from East St. Louis to go on to college in 1990. I believe my grades and test scores were good enough to get me a scholarship to Stanford, MIT, or other elite institutions that sent me their brochures. I knew, though, that I would never have been able to see my family had I not stayed close to home. My mother could not afford to visit me at a campus in another part of the country. She would not have been thrilled to venture too far from East St. Louis anyway. I knew that I would not have any money to come home for the holidays either. I was very fortunate that the University of Illinois (U of I), a fine institution in its own right, was in Champaign, just hours from my home. The school was ranked among the top three engineering schools in the country. When they offered me a full-tuition scholarship to pursue an engineering degree, I jumped at the opportunity.

Fortunately, Harlan got the same deal, so we agreed to go to U of I as roommates. Talk about culture shock! I had been an excellent student in math and science—even won a few district awards—but I was in no shape to compete with the students I met at U of I. I quickly realized the effects of being underprepared in science labs that were "30 to 50 years outdated" (Kozol, 1991, p. 27). The students in my classes were from some of the best schools in the world. I was trained using pictures of chemistry equipment in old textbooks, while these students had grown up with quality teachers, using the best instruments, and working in the best facilities money could buy. It was truly a humbling experience. I certainly had a few excellent teachers in East St. Louis, including Mrs. Thomas, Mr. Poindexter, Mrs. Johnson and Mrs. Massenburg, but the overall quality teaching in these communities has to improve. We must recruit talented individuals, pay them fairly, and provide them with robust training and development—technical training as well as "soft skills" training, such as diversity, teamwork, communication skills, and conflict resolution. They also need better resources. I find it hilarious and irritating when people say that resources are not crucial to ensure a proper education for kids. As I wrote earlier, they say, "You can't throw money at the problem." Yet, they are perfectly fine with sending their kids to schools, particularly private schools that are flush with resources. Remarkably, people send their kids to these schools precisely to give them an advantage over their peers, but later try to downplay that their kids experienced any advantage. I believe that you can't just throw money at the problem, but money is necessary to provide the basic tools, materials, and experiences that promote learning and growth.

As difficult as it was to keep up in the classroom, life was more challenging outside of class. The scholarship only covered tuition and books, which still left living expenses to tackle. Against my academic advisor's wishes, I had to get a job to make up for the shortfall. While I was trying to balance my rigorous classwork with a part-time job to keep the utilities and phone connected (both of which ended up disconnected a couple times), I had neighbors whose parents would send them money and buy them what they needed or often wanted. It is true that not all the White students at Illinois were from well-to-do families, but the overwhelming majority of students living in upscale apartments, eating in great restaurants, driving luxury cars, going to exciting places for spring break and, most importantly, being able to devote their full attention to their studies instead of working to keep the utilities connected, were White.

Harlan and I were desperately looking for ways to make ends meet. We learned during our freshman year that there were some students getting food stamps. While I detested being on food stamps as a kid, I was really at a low point. I convinced myself that the program existed for people like me, someone who just needed some assistance to bridge the time between school and eventual employment upon graduation. Food stamps would be the government's short-term investment in me until I graduated and did not need them anymore—presumably forever. Harlan and I begrudgingly went to the appropriate government office to apply, which already brought back bad memories. After waiting for what seemed like hours, someone called Harlan's name and, a few minutes later, a woman finally called me. She gave me flashbacks of my time at government offices as a kid. The workers always seemed to be irritated that we dared ask for their help, and they always seemed to look down on my mother and me as if we were the scum of the earth. The woman who was supposed to be assisting me fit the description perfectly. Before I even opened my mouth, I could tell from her body language that I was going to be a burden to her. She acted as though she was doing me a favor just by agreeing to meet with me. I reluctantly explained my situation to her. When she heard that I was a college student working a part-time job, she seemed to take great joy in telling me that I did not qualify for the food stamp program. She informed me that I needed to work a certain amount of hours to qualify, and I was currently working under that threshold. Based on my discussion with my adviser, there was no way for me to add any additional work hours and keep up in the classroom.

Getting denied for food stamps stung, but for me, the most infuriating part about the whole experience was the woman's attitude. Her comment to me was, "Well, you chose to go to college, so you have to live with that decision." I could not believe this woman had the nerve to imply that staying home and getting public assistance would have been a better choice for me than going to college. After telling her, "I will come back here in four years after I graduate, and you will still be sitting in this desk," she threatened to get security to walk me out of the place. While I pride myself these days on my expertise in practicing and teaching emotional intelligence (EI), let me just say that the way I reacted was not one of my best displays of EI. Besides the ridiculous assertion that receiving food stamps might have been a better option for me than going to school, the perceived power dynamic at play irked me. The woman's behavior clearly exemplifies the predictable traps into which our vulnerable minds can lead us. Though she was Black and maybe even one paycheck away from being on the other side of her desk, she acted as though she was superior to other Blacks because she had what she thought was a good job even though it was entry-level. One of the challenges with being in an underrepresented group is that the experience often results in low expectations. After all, people in her circle may have been unemployed, so she had already achieved more than they had. She may have asked herself why even aspire to higher levels in the organization? Maybe she had felt unimportant all of her life until she got a job where so many people needed her. Maybe she was jealous that I was going to school and would likely end up with a better career than she had.

What saved me during those financial struggles were my summers at McDonnell Douglas thanks to my involvement with INROADS, established in Chicago in 1970 to, as its mission states, "Develop and place talented minority youth in business and industry and to prepare them for corporate and community leadership." Inspired by Dr. Martin Luther King Jr.'s landmark "I Have a Dream" speech, INROADS founder, Frank C. Carr, quit his executive-level corporate day job and committed to develop a method to increase ethnic diversity of employees in U.S. corporate management by changing the way these candidates gain entry into the business world. INROADS provides ongoing academic support, career training, and guidance to thousands of interns each year (INROADS, 2015). I was fortunate enough to be selected amongst the handful of talented students from East St. Louis to participate in the St. Louis affiliate of INROADS. I interviewed and secured an internship with McDonnell Douglas, which is now part of Boeing, after my senior year in high school. For three additional summers I returned to McDonnell Douglas to work in various engineering departments of the company. These early internship experiences not only introduced me to Corporate America, as Mr. Carr had intended, but that time also shaped my work ethic and sense of responsibility that has served me well throughout my career. I was so proud of my job. I enjoyed getting dressed up in a suit and tie to go to the office while most people my age were wearing uniforms and working at fast-food restaurants. Moreover, I am not sure how I would have survived without the income from those summer jobs.

A TALE OF TWO CAMPUSES

The campus at the University of Illinois was very segregated. The Greek system, which was the largest in the nation at the time, was split along racial lines. I knew of few Black students who were members of predominately White fraternities and sororities. There were separate homecoming functions and student activities for Black students. I was the speaker at my graduation, which was separate from the main graduation ceremony. I am not suggesting the university forced this because students could attend whatever event they wanted, but rather the students requested it because of the historical lack of representation.   Many of the Black students got deeply involved in social justice issues, at least pro-Black causes. There was a tremendous sense of Black pride—at least on the surface, which often manifested itself in a rejection of White America as well as a clear sense of them vs. us. Blacks often criticized Whites for excessive alcohol use and public intoxication, questionable hygiene, over-the-top public displays of affection, and wild sexual behavior. It was easy for me to believe all of these negative stereotypes about Whites because I probably wanted them to be true. I needed them to be true.   When I heard stories that were consistent with those beliefs, I accepted them; when I heard stories that were inconsistent with those beliefs or stories that portrayed Black people this way, I dismissed them. To say I suffered from selective perception, a common trap of our fragile minds, would be an understatement. For the few Black students who dared to spend their time with Whites, Blacks students deemed them as outcasts and sellouts.

We frequently protested what we believed to be unfair campus policies and practices. I can remember standing for hours with dozens of Black students in the bitter cold in front of the university president's office shouting "President Ike; we don't like," referring to then President Stanley O. Ikenberry. We felt he had not taken appropriate action to address some significant racial incidents that occurred on campus.   Consistent with the issues that are playing out in many cities across the U.S., perceived mistreatment by the campus police was a huge issue at the time I was in college. Early on, I jumped on the emotional bandwagon and saw the police as the obvious enemy, but over time, I began to think deeply about these situations. Some of these incidents were clear examples of police bias, but other situations were not as clear. For instance, Black students would complain about never seeing the police parked outside White fraternity parties, yet they were such a familiar sight around the corner from parties that Black students were having. The natural reaction from most of us was hostility toward the police for what seemed like biased treatment. On the other hand, I could see why the police might have wanted to be nearby. Quite a few of our parties ended in fights between individuals, rival fraternities, or a fraternity and the football team. Was this racial bias or good policing?

A NEW MEANING OF BLACK

Although I grew up in an almost completely Black city, it wasn't until my experience at U of I that I gained a broader perspective on what it meant to be Black. Until that point, most of the Black folks I knew were poor. I was now rubbing elbows with Black people, many of whom lived with both parents in safe communities in modern homes. These students had an entirely different worldview than I; they hadn't been beaten up by the trauma of poverty. I enjoyed spending time with people who had different experiences than my own. When I pledged my fraternity, I developed special relationships with ten other young Black men from vastly different backgrounds. It was such a great boost to my optimism, (which, as I will outline later, is one aspect of EI that is critical for resilience), to interact with Black people from higher income levels. I knew that what I had dreamed of was possible because I was meeting people who lived that life.

Not only did my college experience give me more insight into who I was as a Black American, but I ultimately learned to appreciate other cultures. By the time I was a junior, I began to mute some of those old ideas I had about Whites. While I cannot say I developed any meaningful friendships with any non-Black students up to that point, I did interact more directly with people who were not Black. I became the president of the debate team as the only Black team member. I participated in plays where the casts were predominately White. I even occasionally attended parties at White fraternity houses. I began to balance my perception and shake many of the stereotypes that I previously accepted without question. I had several experiences that just didn't fit what I had blindly believed, such as what happened when I worked as a salesperson in the hardware department of the local Sears.

One day, a white-haired White man in a wheelchair rolled up to me and asked for my assistance in making a purchase. I can't remember what he bought, but we struck up a conversation that continued for several minutes and began an interesting relationship. Terry would sometimes come into the store just to see me and talk about random issues—sports, school, whatever. We formed a unique and refreshing bond. He was like a mentor to me. On one hand, here was this older White guy who I might have previously looked at and assumed he was racist. On the other hand, I was a young Black male, who some White people might have automatically stereotyped as a being thug. We both had every reason to have a chip on our shoulders. He had been struck a vicious blow in life that rendered him disabled; I had been struck a vicious blow in life being born as what some people referred to as an endangered species because so many of us were being jailed or murdered. Yet, the two of us were able to connect. About a year after I left the position at Sears, I was in the mall with my family who had scraped up enough money to come to Champaign for my graduation. As we were walking out of a store, someone yelled, "Jarik." It was indeed Terry rolling up in his wheelchair. It had been a while since I had seen him, so I explained to him that I had graduated. His face lit up like that of a proud relative. I could tell that he was genuinely happy for me, despite our racial and age differences.

MY GRADUATE SCHOOL EXPERIENCE

After graduating from U of I, I took a short-term position with the

St. Louis Cardinals, America's greatest baseball franchise, while I waited to hear back from graduate schools to which I had applied. During work one day, I decided to call a few of the schools to get a status update on my applications. Of all the schools that had accepted me, I was most excited about the Cornell University School of Industrial & Labor Relations (ILR). Cornell is perennially the top-rated human resources management program in the nation. Not only had this prestigious Ivy League school accepted me, but they also awarded me a much-needed academic scholarship. I shared my good news with my coworkers, many of whom were White women in their 50s and 60s. When they got wind of my acceptance to Cornell, they took turns hugging and congratulating me. I went home feeling like a million bucks. I burst in the house and shouted to my mother, "I am going to Cornell!" She responded, "Where is it?" I told her that it was in Ithaca, New York. She looked puzzled and asked, "Why do you want to go way over there?" As you can imagine, her response dampened my mood a bit, but the worst was yet to come.

My brother, who spent his days in our basement playing video games, shouted up the stairs, "Just 'cause you are going to Cornell doesn't mean them White folks gonna' give you no job when you get out!" He insisted that I would be right back in East St. Louis looking for odd jobs just like everybody else. I yelled back downstairs, "Since there is a possibility that I might not get a job when I finish school, I should just give up like you did and guarantee that I won't get a job by not finishing school in the first place!" The same brother dropped out of school in the ninth grade. My mother took him to a psychiatrist to figure out why he would not attend. He told the doctor that he dropped out because "their teaching methods are obsolete." The psychiatrist told my mother that my brother was fine. My mother, in the only way she can say it, told the psychiatrist that *he* was the one who was crazy. Despite my mother's concern and my brother's dire warnings, I decided to try Cornell.

While there, I was one of only three Black students in the master's program in the ILR School. Because I wanted to be more well rounded than the average human resources professional, I decided to work on a Master's in Business Administration (MBA) to go along with my ILR degree. There were also only a handful of Blacks in the business school. To stay connected to the Black community, I became active and eventually was elected co-president of the Black Graduate & Professional Student Association (BGPSA). The organization existed precisely for the reason I joined—because there were few opportunities for graduate level students to interact with other Blacks on a regular basis because the numbers on campus were so low.

I found myself participating more than ever in "mainstream" activities at Cornell. Some of the things that seemed so strange to me before were suddenly growing on me. I played poker on the weekends with my ILR classmates instead of the spades or bid whist I played growing up. I went to bars and was sometimes content with drinking and talking as opposed to dancing like I was used to doing on Friday and Saturday nights with my Black friends. My Cornell experience opened my eyes to the world of possibilities previously categorized in my upbringing as "White people's stuff." I drew the line, however, on Thursday nights. Each Thursday night, many of my White classmates would gather to watch *Friends* and *Seinfeld*, while the Black students would get together to watch *Martin Lawrence* and *Living Single*. What was most interesting about this ritual is that my White classmates didn't seem to understand why I wasn't interested in watching *Friends* even though they would not dream of watching *Martin Lawrence*. To them, *Martin Lawrence* was a Black show and Friends was a normal show. This double standard would routinely surface while I was at Cornell. One of my closest friends while there, Anil, is Indian. Anil and I would always marvel at the fact that our White friends expected us to be at events where the crowds were mostly White, but generally declined the opportunity to attend events where they would have been in the minority. We would chuckle at how out of place they seemed when we persuaded them to attend either a function with a majority Indian or majority Black crowd. These were future human resources professionals, mind you, who would probably be responsible at some point in their careers for leading the diversity efforts of their employers. They were good guys by the way—it's just that many of them had lived segregated lives like I had. I was forced to adapt if I wanted to be successful; however, they didn't have to do so. The only time Whites were in the minority was when they proactively chose those activities. I, on the other hand, had to proactively seek out activities where I wouldn't be in the minority.

Though there were a few challenges, I really enjoyed my classmates at the ILR school. The situation at the Johnson School of Business was much more uncomfortable. For the most part, my ILR faculty and my fellow students seemed like they cared about me and wanted me to feel included. I did not feel included in the business school culture. The students did not make an effort to connect with me, so I didn't work hard to connect with them. It seemed that many of them were dealing with a bit of insecurity since the school was only ranked eighth in the country at the time, and many of them had gotten rejected from the top three schools. I spent my free time with my now wife, Adrienne, who was a student at the Law School, and with my ILR classmates, who were all comforted by the fact that we were at the top ranked ILR school in the world.

AFTER COLLEGE: BECOMING AMERICAN

Fortunately, I have had countless experiences that have challenged my old ways of thinking. It has not been easy, but both the highs and lows have been richly rewarding. Once I graduated from Cornell, I accepted a position with Citibank, primarily because of their robust human resources management development program. Citibank rotated me to Stamford, Connecticut for nine months and then to Chicago for nine months. For my final rotation in the program, Adrienne and I spent six months living in Dublin, Ireland. We enjoyed our Dublin experience immensely. Neither one of us had ever been abroad, but during those six months, we traveled every time there was a bank holiday—and because of the different views on work-life balance than in the U.S., there were plenty of bank holidays.

Now that I could walk in the footsteps of great leaders, artists, and thinkers from the majestic Pantheon in Rome to the opulent Palace of Versailles, I wished that I had listened more in history class. All of a sudden, this stuff had meaning to me because I could see it and touch it. We visited Spain and England. I went to the Netherlands. We traveled throughout Italy by train. I can remember sitting in a gondola in Venice thinking about East St. Louis and wishing my family could experience this, but they did not even come to visit me in Dublin because they said they were afraid of flying "over all of that water." I know it was much deeper than that; they were terrified at the prospect of being in such a different culture. I have to admit that my wife and I had some particular concerns about being Black in a country that does not have many Black citizens, an estimated at a little over 1 percent of residents (Central Statistics Office, 2011).

During this time, I really understood what it meant to be American. First Lady Michelle Obama got much backlash for making a similar statement, but the truth is that television programs, newspaper reports, and my own experiences growing up constantly reminded me that I was Black, an "other" in America. Abroad, however, people seemed to regard us as Americans first, as opposed to being Black. Because people generally held America in high regard in all the places we visited, I was no longer an "other" or "underdog," but suddenly part of the favored team. People would walk up to us in restaurants and ask if we were American, and they wanted to know what part of America we lived. Instead of following us to make sure we didn't steal anything as is often the case in the U.S., storeowners' eyes lit up when we walked into their stores because they knew we were American and assumed we were willing to spend significantly. I was glued to the television to watch Justin Leonard sink that long birdie putt on 17 to tie the match and propel that thrilling come from behind win by the U.S. Ryder Cup Team against Europe in 1999. I was so proud walking around the office the next day.

When I returned to America I was reminded in subtle and not so subtle ways that I am not really part of the favored team. One vivid reminder was learning from my neighbors and friends about Axe Handle Saturday, which that had occurred in 1960 in my new city, Jacksonville, Florida. Black youth who were attempting a sit-in at a local lunch counter were attacked by an angry mob of Whites swinging axe handles. While our education and experience have opened many doors for my wife and me professionally in Jacksonville, race continues to be an issue of concern for us, particularly now that we have kids. We desperately want things to be better for them as they grow up. As a human resources professional, I was involved in resolving countless conflicts involving race, so it has always been at the front of my mind. My wife, as a labor and employment attorney, routinely deals with issues of race. We have both witnessed how deeply seeded these issues can be, and we are frequently reminded that there is much work to be done for the country to improve.

KEEPING IT REAL

I love being Black. There are some interesting and fun customs and traditions that are unique to Blacks. I feel comfortable approaching Black people in any city in America.   If I am in a crowded room and spot another Black person, I'll give him or her a head nod in acknowledgement. There is a certain connection that comes with shared experiences for anyone, particularly for people who are members of a subgroup.   For instance, I have talked to educational leaders who are troubled by the fact the Black kids want to sit together in the cafeteria at lunchtime. This is such a common occurrence that there is a book about it, *Why Are All the Black Kids Sitting Together in the Cafeteria?* (Tatum, 2003). This is one of the many situations where I think the country struggles with understanding metaphors - "how this situation is like that situation." In other words, people can understand behavior in one context, but struggle to understand the same behavior if the context is slightly different. Black kids want to sit with other Black kids in the cafeterias of predominantly

White schools for the same reason that you will be drawn to someone wearing a sweatshirt bearing the name of your hometown if you are on an international vacation somewhere. Chances are you will walk up to that person and strike up a conversation. It is a natural thing to desire to connect with someone who shares something with you. Those connections become magnified when you are in a subgroup. If you are in Michigan, for example, a University of Michigan sweatshirt would barely catch your eye, but you would notice it right away in Venice, Italy.

While I have a "natural" connection to Black people through culture, I am troubled by some of what Black culture takes for granted. The problem isn't just what we do, but also what we don't do. Playing golf, jogging, swimming, and relaxing at the beach—all activities that were foreign to me growing up—are now a part of my immediate family's lifestyle. Experiencing new cultures and customs has become a theme for my family. Learning about other cultures has also helped us to further understand our own. Everything from the foods we eat, to the places we go, to the music we listen to has changed. Many of my friends and family still in the East St. Louis area would say that I have "sold out." The problem is not that I have changed; the problem is that the people criticizing me haven't changed. To me, authentic change implies learning, progress, growth, and maturity. The misguided view some people have about "keeping it real" is a substantial barrier to progress. For instance, one summer when my folks came to Florida to visit me, I decided to grill some food for the whole gang. Today, my wife, kids, and I practice a whole food plant-based diet, which means we eat no animal products, but at the time my kids weren't born yet and my wife and I were vegetarians. Being a good host, I didn't want to pressure them to only eat only vegetables, so I bought and grilled a bunch of meat and seafood for them. After I placed the last pieces of meat on the grill, I added a handful of asparagus. Once the food was ready, I placed it on a platter and brought it into the house. I then went to clean off the grill. When I returned, the platter was picked clean, well, all except for the asparagus and a piece or two of meat that was touching the asparagus. I guess they didn't want asparagus juice on their hamburgers. They avoided it because we didn't grow up eating asparagus; it didn't matter that it was a tasty, healthy option. Keep in mind that my family has dealt with all kinds of major health crises. By the time of their visit, I had already lost one sister to cancer at age 35. Soon after their visit, I lost another sister at age 48 to a heart attack. My mother would later say about our plant-based diets, "Y'all are eating like them," referring to Whites.

Going Back "Home"

From the moment that I enter the East St. Louis airspace, I am overwhelmed with mixed emotions. The city made me who I am, and I have a strong emotional connection to it. There is something special about many of the people there, but on the other hand, I am profoundly sad that so many young people are still there struggling. The city is different from any place I have lived since I left. I joke with my friends and family that it feels like entering a third-world country when I return after being away for a while. I see the same predictable sights, and I am reminded that a degree of apathy has invaded parts of "Black America." Apathy is caused by emotional overload, a feeling that the task is so monumental that any individual effort would be wasted. No matter how challenging it is to live in a particular community, these people could not imagine life outside of their hometown. They often have little self-regard, and they have little interest in education because they do not envision much resulting from going to school. They feel that the life they were born into is the life they are destined to live and become complacent, viewing success only in terms of others around them. Having a child at 16 years old is not so bad when all of your friends had theirs at 14. Making a D in a class is not so bad when several people failed. It is a human phenomenon, not just an inner-city phenomenon, to use those around you to gauge your success. People in this situation often suffer from undiagnosed depression and other mental illnesses that ignite and perpetuate their downward spiral.

Given the data that I present in this book regarding the poor quality of life for Blacks, for so many people in these situations, they perceive "real" success as being stamped "for Whites only."

One of the most common examples of the apathy I have witnessed is a morbidly obese, scantily clad, pregnant, single mother pushing a stroller with a couple of toddlers following close behind. She has just returned from the nail salon where she spent a significant portion of her welfare check getting her hair, nails, and makeup done. She is on her cell phone, searching for a babysitter to keep the kids while she goes to the club to party tonight. She puts her friend on hold and yells to one of the kids, "You ain't shit. You ain't never going to be shit, just like your daddy." It is sad that she will likely never make it out of East St. Louis, but what is more sad is that her kids probably won't either. It is easy to be angry and judgmental, but it is important to remember that she was just a kid herself not long ago; she has little idea of what to do differently than her parents did with her.

It's Not Just East St. Louis

I am writing this section on a plane to Denver from Atlanta. At the Atlanta airport, while sitting in one of the food court areas, I decided to imagine that I had just stepped off of a plane arriving in America for the first time. I realize that this is no scientific study, but for about 20 minutes, I simply made note of what I saw. What would that food court tell me about race relations in America?

I saw enough hair weave and dye to fill a beauty supply store. The vast majority of workers at the fast food restaurants were Black. Black ladies working as cashiers, Black men and women working as cooks. One guy cleaning up the food court was Black, the other Latino. I saw two young Black males with dreadlocks walking around wearing sunglasses indoors. Each of the baggage handlers was a Black male. One of them walked with an exaggerated lean to emphasize how cool he felt he was. There was a Black man playing piano to entertain the travelers as they scarfed down their meals between flights. All of the pilots and the majority of the flight attendants who scurried by were White. Other than me, I saw only a couple of Black males wearing business suits. I don't recall seeing a Black female in business attire. I have to admit that given what I saw, my view of Black people would not be very positive. I would have known immediately that this was the group on the lower economic rung. It would likely have seemed to me that the primary role of Blacks was to serve and entertain Whites. I saw disheveled Whites who looked like they were struggling economically as well, but they were scattered among the hordes of professionally attired Whites passing through.

I don't want to pick on Atlanta. Keep in mind that Atlanta is one of the most progressive cities in the country for Blacks. I spent a summer there while in graduate school. I loved the city and my experiences there. One of my most distinct memories is going into my supervisor's neighborhood after work one evening. I was impressed with the homes and I was curious to know how many Black people lived in the neighborhood. I was shocked to hear him tell me that virtually the entire neighborhood was Black. He pointed to one of the smallest homes and indicated that it was where the lone White family lived. That experience left such an impression on me that I called home to tell my mother. However, even in a place like Atlanta, the race problems in America were evident in the food court at the airport. In fact, visit the airport in Any City, USA and you are likely to encounter the same caste-like system. While things have certainly gotten better over the past 10 years, there still appears to be a racial stratification resulting in the shoeshine folks, janitors, fast food workers (except for the managers), and baggage handlers being disproportionately Black, while the ticket agents, pilots, and flight attendants are disproportionately White.

This book is about addressing the fact that Whites—who are looking to wipe their hands clean of the problems Blacks are experiencing—will accept the behavior of the young lady in East St. Louis as absolutely true for most Blacks. They will respond to my description of what I saw at the Atlanta airport as proof that the problem is with Blacks themselves as opposed to any sort of racism. Blacks who are looking to blame everything on someone else will be highly offended and defensive about what I have described. This book is about bridging this divide. What is clear to me is that the answers to questions of Black and White are seldom black and white. Our emotional racial debates make it difficult for us to remember that people aren't all good or bad, right or wrong. We are at once all of those things and none of those things. People tend to react to symptoms as opposed to the root causes undergirding the issues. Simple solutions like saying all Whites are racist or Black people just need to pull up their pants and try harder are naive and dangerous. This argument embarrasses some people, infuriates others, and renders many people hopeless. I am not interested in making excuses for people. I am interested discovering legitimate, data-driven, psychological reasons why people behave the way they do.

SUMMARY

In sharing my life experiences with you, I am aware that I represent merely a data point. I am an outlier in many ways. The hard fact for people to understand is that no single one of us can solve anything solely based on our own personal experiences. Limited and often misleading personal stories and reflections fail to make appropriate connections to what researchers have learned about human behavior en masse. On the other hand, we too often read publications from trained professionals who have the technical knowledge but lack the real-world experience in the phenomena about which they write. Without that life experience to contextualize the information they study, their work is limited as well. *The Fragile Mind* represents my attempt to blend my personal experience with what I have learned about the science of human behavior into a practical framework that parents, elected officials, law enforcement personnel, educators, employers, and nonprofit leaders can use to deal more effectively with issues of race.

Why should any of this matter to you if you are not Black? Besides the basic issue of fairness, ask yourself how America can compete with emerging economies, such as China and India, if already large and increasingly growing pockets of our population in places like East St. Louis can hardly contend with the difficulties of daily life, let alone excel in Science, Technology, Engineering, and Math (STEM). Lack of skills renders many people of color helpless and sitting on the bench at a time when America needs its entire team on the field because America's millennials are struggling. According to the Program for the International Assessment of Adult Competencies (PIAAC), America's millennials posted an average score of 274 on 500-point scale in literacy, while the average among participating countries is 282. We tied for last place in numeracy, an average score of 255, while the average for participating countries was 275 on a 500-point scale (Zinshteyn, 2015). The lack of adequate preparation translates into tens of thousands of unfilled jobs. Without figuring out how to engage people of color who are falling by the wayside, America may be an afterthought of the global landscape in the not-so-distant future.

CHAPTER 2

A Lesson in Hypocrisy: The Immigrant Experience

A fully functional multiracial society
cannot be achieved without
a sense of history and open, honest dialogue.
—Dr. Cornel West

American history is littered with wild hypocrisies, particularly regarding race relations. I have written in this book primarily about the Black American experience because I have lived it, but groups from all over the world have had immense challenges as they began their American experience. Native Americans and early immigrants from places such as Mexico, China, Japan, Ireland, as well as Jewish immigrants from all over the world, have played a pivotal role in developing the country and creating the enormous wealth that America enjoys today. These early burden-bearers of America were sometimes stolen from their native lands, sometimes pushed out of their homes because of wars, sometimes compelled to leave their birth places to escape famine, and sometimes inspired to leave in search of the "American Dream." For whatever reason, they came, and the arrival of these groups would set the stage for a series of interracial conflicts that would serve the interests of the elite class, forming the foundation for the current racial disparities we see in America.

WELCOME TO AMERICA

The Native American Experience

Not only were the natives already here when Christopher Columbus arrived, but he and his crew were not even the first explorers to travel to the "New World." Leif Eriksson and his Vikings had already visited five hundred years before Columbus got here in 1492. Yet, we still celebrate Columbus for his "discovery." In his book, *A Different Mirror*, Ronald Takaki points out that Columbus wrote regarding his early experience with Native Americans, "They do not bear arms or know them" (Takaki, 1993, p. 31). Columbus described Native Americans as being "very gentle and without knowledge of […] evil." He wrote, "They love their neighbors as themselves, and have the sweetest talk in the world, and gentle, and always with a smile" (Takaki, p. 32). Despite his kind description, Columbus and his men proceeded to murder and kidnap Native Americans, rape the women, and use that very innocence he wrote about against them. In 1493, he gathered 550 Native Americans to take back to Europe with him and watched 200 die at sea. His crew tossed them overboard like garbage (Takaki, 1993).

In the early 1600s, Native Americans were responsible for the survival of many of the first colonists who had been forced to eat dogs, cats, rats, shoes, and mice to stave off starvation. Some accounts suggest that they dug up and ate human corpses and even resorted to cannibalism (Associated Press, 2013). The Powhatans came to their aid with food. The colonists soon grew strong enough to attack that same tribe and destroy their villages. The early settlers also brought catastrophic disease. Between 1610 and 1675, the Native American population declined sharply because of diseases they acquired from the colonists —nearly 80% reduction for some tribes (Takaki, 1993).

Because of Native Americans' different customs and beliefs, colonists didn't have a positive view of them. The root cause of much of the colonists' anxiety was the fact that their children were starting to take on some of the characteristics of the Native Americans, which the colonists interpreted as a threat to their civility. Our beloved founding father Thomas Jefferson took an approach in early America to ensure this kind of "assault" on the social order by Native Americans did not happen. Jefferson saw only two options for the Native Americans, "Be civilized or exterminated" (Takaki, 1993, p. 47). Becoming civilized meant assimilating, or becoming White.

To assimilate would prove a difficult task for the Native Americans because many of their values stood in stark contrast to those of the colonists. For instance, the colonists believed the Native Americans were squandering the land by not farming it to its maximum capacity. Colonists ultimately convinced themselves that it was their divine duty to take Native American lands for their own—Manifest Destiny. To speed up this process, Native Americans were put on reservations in the 1850s. The 1862 Homestead Act provided incentives for squatters to invade Indian lands in the Midwest.

Lawmakers passed the Native American Appropriations Act in 1871, leading to the destruction of the political existence of the tribes, which made it easier to try to force assimilation (Takaki, 1993). Tribal relations were further crippled by the 1887 Dawes Act, which broke up collectively owned Indian lands and redistributed it to individuals, resulting in "surplus" land being sold to Whites. Jefferson admitted that purchases of Native American lands were "sometimes made with the price in one hand and the sword in the other" (Takaki, 1993, p. 47). Lewis Cass, Secretary of War under President Jackson, summed up 19th-century Indian policy this way: "The Indians are entitled to the enjoyment of all the rights which do not interfere with the obvious designs of Providence" (Brunner, & Rowen, 2007). Meanwhile, there were boarding schools established all over the country such as the one in Carlisle, Pennsylvania, where its founder, army officer Richard Henry Pratt, was on a mission to "kill the Indian and save the man." Whites thought this could only be achieved through teaching Native Americans English, converting them to Christianity, and giving them a trade (Churchill, 2004, p. 88). Native Americans never recovered.

Today, Native Americans are largely forgotten, except for in the world of sports. The debate over the name Washington Redskins has heated up in recent years. Many Americans stress that team names, logos, and mascots are meant to honor Native Americans. Few people in the debate have knowledge of the historical context of the Washington football team. Washington, the only pro football team south of the Mason-Dixon line at the time, wanted to attract southern fans. The song "Fight for Old D.C." used to be "Fight for Old Dixie" (Peterson, n.d.). Moreover, Washington was the last pro football team to integrate, which happened fifteen years after all other teams had integrated, and even then under intense pressure from the Kennedy administration. The American Nazi Party and Ku Klux Klan even marched outside the stadium in support of the team remaining White only (Zirin & Zill, 2011). Some people claim the name "redskin" is a reference to bloody scalps; others suggest the origins of the word "redskin" had nothing to do with bloody scalps, but rather a term of endearment that Native Americans used with each other. It is important to note that the lyrics of "Fight for old D.C.!" used to include "Scalp 'em, swamp 'em." Those words were later changed to "Beat 'em, swamp 'em!" I have no doubt that the average Washington football fan does not intend to demean Native Americans when they support that team, but that does not make it any less disparaging. Similarly, I am sure that many people who love the Confederate Flag are not hateful racists, but Dylann Ruff proved that some are. Just as it is difficult for many Blacks to look at that flag and not see hate, it is difficult for some Native Americans to look at the Washington mascot and not feel bad about how some people feel about them.

From a practical perspective, the traditional war attire depicted in logos and on mascots provides a one-sided picture of who Native American are. To understand the impact that these names have on our perceptions of Native Americans, all one has to do is ask a child to draw an "American Indian." I would bet the kid would draw a figure in a headdress, wearing war paint, and carrying spears. As such, these team names and images minimize the richness and fullness of the Native American culture Some Native Americans think that the mascots are acceptable, but this is of little consequence, particularly if they have financial incentives at stake. After all, there were Africans who sold other Africans into slavery. Moreover, there were slaves who, once they learned of their freedom after emancipation, responded, "We ain't gonna' leave masta." I am sure very few people would justify slavery because some Blacks have engaged in this behavior.

It is certainly possible that, while the first owner of the team was openly hostile towards Blacks, he may have felt more positive about Native Americans. It is also easy to see, however, how a racist could have animus towards all nonwhite groups. While the Washington Redskin issue is still debatable, what is unambiguous is the eradication of Native American culture that occurred at the hands of early Americans. A common defense of poor treatment of Native Americans is that nations conquered other nations all the time. People have always fought to acquire more land and extend their territories, but we at least have to be honest and admit that our actions do not demonstrate that we care about Native Americans at all. Below is the snapshot of Native American's today (Hair, 2014).

- Dropout rates for Native American students are nearly triple the rates of their white peers, and the percentage of young adults from ages 25-34 who hold a bachelor's degree is less than half the national average, 12% compared to 31%, respectively.

- As of 2012, the median household income of single-race American Indian and Alaska Native households was $35,310, over 30% less than the national median of $51,371.

- Unemployment for Native Americans has remained above 10%, substantially higher than the national average.

- While the national poverty rate was 15.9% in 2012, 29.1% of single-race American Indians and Alaska Natives lived below the poverty line.

- From 2001-2008, food insecurity in the Native American community fluctuated between 23% and 42%, consistently above the national average.

The Mexican Experience

Imagine going to sleep in one country, but waking up in another. This is what happened to Mexicans after fighting the Mexican-American War from 1846 to 1848. The war was prompted by the annexation of Texas as part of Manifest Destiny, the same idea that was used to cripple the Native Americans. Every time Mexicans thought they had an agreement with Americans, the borders were changed. Mexicans found themselves trading in their cowboy work, a system that they invented, for unskilled labor positions that paid them less than what Whites were making for the same jobs. The development of the railroad accelerated the movement of Mexicans to the United States. For example, in the 1920s, Mexicans comprised 85% of the agricultural labor in Texas compared to 10% for Whites and 5 percent for Blacks (Takaki, 1993). In a theme that would echo the experiences of many early immigrant groups, Mexicans were often used as strikebreakers to pit minority groups against each other, or to keep the White labor class in check. As with many of these early groups, Mexicans entered into contracts that in effect made them slaves by driving up their debt to amounts that they could never pay off. They relied on their employers for all of their needs—food, household items, etc. Their "employers" set the prices and controlled the wages to serve their own interests. During the Great Depression, Mexican laborers became targets of repatriation programs because they were thought to have taken jobs away from Whites. These programs forced Mexicans, many of whom were legal U.S. citizens, to live in Mexico.

The current debate about illegal immigration harkens back to the early class wars that evolved into race wars in the United States. So much ire is directed at immigrants who enter the country illegally. While there are legitimate policy debates, to some people there seems to be a visceral hatred directed toward illegal immigrants (especially from Mexico) spurred on by politicians seeking votes. The immigration issue is another emotional problem that perfectly illustrates the vulnerabilities of our fragile minds. First, hundreds of thousands of would-be illegal immigrants are arrested each year before they make it across the border. A record high of 1.6 million people was arrested in 2000 and 420,000 in 2013 (Associated Press, 2014). Of those who slip past border security, hundreds die each year from drowning, heat strokes, and other causes while making the trek from Mexico to cross the 2,000-mile border in search of better opportunities for their families. The total number of people who died crossing the US-Mexico border was 445 in 2013 and 307 in 2014 (Sanders, 2014). Many of the dead are never identified because of the severe decomposition of the bodies. Imagine what that does to families, particularly families who are already living in traumatic poverty.

There is no denying that illegal immigrants have broken the law to get here, so they are technically criminals. However, despite 2016 presidential candidate Donald Trump's inflammatory comments, "They're bringing drugs. They're bringing crime. They're rapists," it is doubtful that a significant number of immigrants risk there lives to come here to murder, rape, or steal (Bump, 2015). There is no definitive data on crime rates among illegal immigrants. Even the pro low-immigration group, Center for Immigration Studies, indicate that, "The overall picture of immigrants and crime remains confused due to a lack of good data and contrary information" (Camarota and Vaughan, 2009). Within any population there will be bad seeds, but the vast majority of immigrants come to America to work. Despite the relatively low pay, they can earn more in a few days here than they can earn in weeks in Mexico. Those who are lucky enough to make it here live in the shadows because they know they have broken the law by crossing the border and they don't want to be caught and ultimately sent back to the situation they ran away from in the first place. Think about that knot you get in the pit of your stomach when you are going above the speed limit on the freeway and see a police car out of the corner of your eye. That unsettling feeling is what many of these people must live with each day, not only when they are at construction sites working on rooftops, but also as they shop in the grocery stores, fill up their cars at gas stations, and play with their kids at the park. In many cases, these are people who have never broken the law in their lives. For some of them, the very pressure of living in the shadows might put them in situations that increase the likelihood of dangerous illegal behavior. They have to cut corners to get things done as opposed to going through the routine protocols of American citizens. One of the most controversial issues regarding illegal immigration is the question of offspring. Children born in the United States are citizens even if their parents are illegal immigrants. Think about what happens to kids of parents that have been caught and deported—foster care, forced adoption, or worse.

Talk shows are filled with pundits ranting about not granting amnesty to these illegal immigrants because it contradicts the American value system. Who are the real beneficiaries when we look the other way? Certainly, the illegal immigrants have some culpability here, but we should ask ourselves why they are here in the first place. How can the companies that employ illegal workers get off the hook? Is this not a form of amnesty? Labor issues have often been at the center of racial/ethnic conflicts. Slavery was about free labor, and some of today's undocumented workers are enduring a near-slavery form of "cheap" labor. Just as the planter elites pitted Blacks against working-class Whites, today's business owners are pitting illegal immigrants against working-class Americans. Just as the Black workers drew the anger of Whites, the illegal immigrants are drawing the ire of the working class, Black and White. Business owners who are exploiting these illegal workers at the expense of working-class Americans share a great deal of culpability; they are criminals for aiding and abetting so-called criminals. The fact is that as long as there is opportunity to make more money than they could in Mexico, people will continue to risk their lives to come here.

While I am a huge proponent of cultural diversity in America, I believe we absolutely need to tighten the borders until we can get things right for the folks who were born here and are suffering from horrible disparities. As of the writing of this book, there is a fierce political debate over the executive action taken by President Obama that would offer protections for over 4 million undocumented immigrants who are already here. Today, the typical undocumented immigrant, more than half of whom are from Mexico, has been living in the United States for over 12 years (Ehrenfreund, 2014). I cannot speak for the legality of the President's actions, but I agree that something had to be done about this problem and its effect on real people.

The Chinese Experience

British Opium Wars and harsh economic conditions initially compelled Chinese people to migrate to America. Chinese people eagerly joined the "gold rush," but soon learned that not being White came with penalties. For Chinese immigrants, these penalties took the form of targeted taxes. Like all laborers in America at the time, Chinese immigrants played a pivotal role in the expansion of the railroad, even though they suffered widespread pay discrimination and were forced to work under abysmal conditions. When White workers began to complain about Chinese immigrants taking jobs from them, Chinese immigrants were systematically expelled from the labor force. They were forced to flee to the Chinatowns on the coasts where they were isolated from the rest of the population, making it difficult to integrate into mainstream society (Wei, n.d.). Moreover, the Chinese Exclusion Act was passed in 1882 to prohibit further Chinese immigration to America. This law was the first to prohibit entry to America based on nationality. According to the U.S. Department of State, Office of the Historian, the law was introduced because:

Many of the non-Chinese workers in the United States came to resent the Chinese laborers, who might squeeze them out of their jobs. Furthermore, as with most immigrant communities, many Chinese settled in their own neighborhoods, and tales spread of Chinatowns as places where large numbers of Chinese men congregated to visit prostitutes, smoke opium, or gamble. Some advocates of anti-Chinese legislation therefore argued that admitting the Chinese into the United States lowered the cultural and moral standards of American society. Others used a more overtly racist argument for limiting immigration from East Asia and expressed concern about the integrity of American racial composition ("Chinese Immigration and the Chinese Exclusion Acts," n.d.).

Having few other options, Chinese immigrants began opening small businesses that performed work that nobody else wanted to do, such as laundries. The Chinese Exclusion Acts were not repealed until 1943 to appease an ally during World War II. The Immigration Act of 1965 repealed the national origins quota system that had been established earlier. As of the 2010 Census, Chinese Americans represented the largest and oldest ethnic group of Asian Americans, comprising 25.9% of the Asian American population. There were 3.8 million Chinese Americans in 2010 (U.S. Census Bureau, 2010). Over half of Chinese Americans are still concentrated in California or New York, and entrepreneurship is still a significant aspect of their culture (Hooper, & Batalova, 2015).

The Japanese Experience

Unlike China, the government organized the transport of selected Japanese to America. The typical profile of a Japanese immigrant was healthy and literate with good political connections. Between 1886 and 1911, more than 400,000 men and women left Japan for the U.S. and U.S. controlled lands, and significant emigration from Japan continued for at least a decade beyond that (Library of Congress, n.d.). Japanese immigration resulted in two distinct experiences.

One experience was the Pacific Coast experience. The people who came to the Pacific Coast were often denied access to employment in the industrial labor market, so they, like Chinese immigrants, became entrepreneurs. Japanese immigrants were particularly gifted in agriculture. By 1920, Japanese immigrant farmers controlled more than 450,000 acres of land in California, brought to market more than 10% of its crop revenue, and had produced at least one American-made millionaire. They had become so successful that some states, including California, enacted practices and legislation that limited Japanese immigration and excluded Japanese immigrants from owning and leasing land. According to the Library of Congress (n.d.):

In 1908, the Japanese and American governments arrived at what became known as the "Gentlemen's Agreement." Japan agreed to limit emigration to the U.S., while the U.S. granted admission to the wives, children, and other relatives of immigrants already resident. Five years later, the California legislature passed the Alien Land Law, which barred all aliens ineligible for citizenship, and therefore all Asian immigrants, from owning land in California, even land they had purchased years before (p. 2).

The attitude toward Japanese immigrants had changed little by WWII when the government put Japanese in internment camps but not the Germans or Italians who we were also fighting. By the end of the war in 1945, 125,000 people, half of them children, had spent up to four years in concentration camps. The evacuees were required to sell their houses, farms, stores, and restaurants, often for pennies on the dollar, before registering with authorities and being sent to the camps. The conditions in these camps were brutal. People died as a result of having no medical attention to deal with their illnesses. The camps were remote facilities with barbed wire fences and armed guards, who would actually shoot people who tried to escape. After the war, Japanese Americans had to endure the challenge of starting from scratch to regain their economic footing. They won some legislative battles, but it wasn't until much later that they received partial compensation for their losses. In 1988, U.S. President Ronald Reagan signed the Civil Liberties Act of 1988 that provided financial redress of $20,000 for each surviving detainee (WJCT, n.d.).

Some Japanese settled in Hawaii. Fruit and sugar plantation owners recruited Japanese people to Hawaii to work with Chinese, Filipino, Korean, Portuguese, and Black laborers. As had been the pattern on the mainland, business owners often pitted these workers against each other to maintain control. In 1853, indigenous Hawaiians made up 97% of the islands' population, but by 1923, they made up only 16%, and the largest percentage of Hawaii's population was Japanese (Library of Congress, n.d.). Work on the plantations was grueling, and Japanese lives were controlled on and off the job. Much like slavery on the mainland, business owners employed European American overseers as enforcers of their strict rules. Japanese workers were legally bound to three- and five-year contracts, but many, despite the risk of being caught and jailed, fled to the mainland before their contracts were up.

The Jewish Experience

The first group of Jewish immigrants fled from Brazil in 1654 when the country was taken over by the Portuguese (Diner, 2004). They were greeted less than enthusiastically because their poverty was thought to pose a burden. In the 1700s, many of the Jewish people in America were of Spanish and Portuguese origin, but they came from many countries. From 1820 to 1924 Jewish immigrants flocked to the "land of opportunity" to escape economic hardship, persecution, and social and political upheaval in their homelands (Library of Congress, n.d.). Merchants and artisans were followed by a wave of peddlers who were later followed by a wave of garment workers. The largest early phase of immigration did not occur until the 1880s from Russia and its neighboring countries.

Like Japanese immigrants who came to the mainland, many of the Jewish people who came to America were already skilled and highly educated. Like no other immigrant group before them, however, Jewish immigrants became intently focused on assimilation. They changed their names, lost their accents, and did everything they could to fit into the mainstream, which could be achieved because of their white skin. Before World War II, Jewish immigrants still faced a great degree of anti-Semitism. For instance, Jewish students were entering Harvard at such a high rate in 1922 that the school's President, Lawrence Lowell, proposed quota's to curb their enrollment (Karabel, 2006). Although his admissions committee rejected that proposal, they did approve other policies that would have the same effect including the requirement to submit photos with applications, preferential treatment towards children of alumni, and more subjective admissions standards (Karabel, 2006). In 1924, the 1882 Chinese Exclusion Act was broadened to lessen Jewish immigration as well (Takaki, 1993). During World War II, many believed that the American government did little to respond to the Holocaust until 1944, with the establishment of the War Refugee Board (WRB) ("United States policy toward Jewish refugees, 1941 - 1952," 2014). By 1952, 137,450 Jewish refugees, including close to 100,000 who had been displaced by the Holocaust, had settled in the United States. Jewish immigrants engaged in chain migration, in which one member of an extended family secured a place in America and then arranged for other family members to come and settle in the country (Hyman, n.d.).

———

The Irish Experience

Learning of the Irish American experience was quite eye opening for me. I had not understood the suffering from which they were fleeing nor the suffering they endured upon arrival to the "promised land" until I read Takaki's book. People primarily left Ireland to escape starvation brought on by the potato famine. While they reluctantly yet voluntarily came over as opposed to being captured and forced here, their passage was similar to African slaves. They came over in disease-riddled, tight-quartered ships. Upon their arrival, Irish immigrants occupied the bottom rungs in the labor market. The Irish were described as the "pioneers of the American ghetto" (Takaki, 1993, p. 9). Even though many of them had denounced the institution of slavery and had empathized with and supported Blacks while in Ireland, they lashed out at Blacks in America after being pitted against them by the White elite.

The Irish, however, soon made great strides. By the early 1900s, Irish Americans were attending college in greater proportions than their American counterparts. They had some help, though. I don't mean to pick on Harvard, but its president pushed for the assimilation of the Irish because of their "similarities" to those of English origin (Takaki, 1993). The Irish were ultimately helped most by having the right to vote. Through suffrage, once their numbers grew, the Irish were able to gain political and economic power by using preferential treatment to award jobs and contracts to their compatriots. They were able to overcome their stereotypes and early mistreatment relatively quickly given the fact that they did not have the same legal barriers as other groups because of their white skin.

SUMMARY

The debate about what information should be included about the country's history in textbooks has surfaced again in America. There are some who suggest that pointing out past injustices carried out by

Americans is unpatriotic. They argue that pointing out the flaws of some of our most revered political figures, for instance, is destructive and threatening to American exceptionalism. My own view is that it is a fool who cannot look in the mirror and point out areas of imperfection. For all the greatness that America has attained, it cannot escape its history and the legacy of this early treatment of its ethnic citizens, particularly because those early experiences set the foundation for the racial strife the people of color experience today.

Nobody in America today should feel angry, guilty, or ashamed about the policies and practices of the government or the behavior of Americans in the 1700s and 1800s. The purpose of being honest about the country's history—good, bad, and in between—is to learn from it, which we have not yet done to the greatest extent possible. Knowing our country's history is necessary to avoid repeating some of the mistakes of our past. If we let our emotions prevent us from admitting our mistakes, we will miss the opportunity to understand how we could have made those mistakes in the first place. The answers to today's most vexing issues regarding race and class can be found by studying the well-established patterns of behavior demonstrated toward each group of new Americans when they first arrived. Native Americans had their country taken, and Mexican Americans, Chinese Americans, Japanese Americans, Jewish Americans, and Irish Americans, among other groups, endured very difficult challenges in their pursuit of the American Dream, which was in many ways "for Whites only." In many instances, people in these groups tried everything they could to be accepted as White. There were even court cases in the nineteenth and early twentieth centuries that determined who was White and who wasn't for the purposes of naturalized citizenship and its associated benefits. The first such case was that of Ah Yup, who argued, unsuccessfully, that Chinese people were White (Lopez, 1997). Other plaintiffs, including Native Americans, Hawaiians, Japanese, Mexicans, and mixed-race persons also failed in their attempts to attain White "status." Syrians, Armenians, and Asian Indians were among the groups with more favorable rulings (Lopez, 1997). Race, not hard work, was the biggest predictor of success in early America - and many wanted to keep it that way.

The cycle is clear and unambiguous:

(1) Except for Native Americans, a new group of ethnic immigrants would arrive in search of a better life for themselves and their families;

(2) Business owners would hire them for less than their current workers and have them work under more difficult conditions;

(3) The displaced workers would get upset with the new immigrants for taking or threatening to take their jobs, treat them poorly, and use their political influence to get politicians to sponsor and pass legislation to limit the number of people from that ethnic group who could come to America.

(4) In every case, including the Native Americans, there was a perceived threat to the social fabric of the country posed by these "lesser" groups. There was always a vigorous fight to maintain the status quo that disproportionately benefitted the elites who were pulling all the strings.

Money may not be the root of all evil, but it is certainly the root of this evil system. The Planter Elite used slavery, a system that continued free labor, to amass fortunes. Later, business owners kept wages low, pitting workers against each other to keep as much profit as possible. Today, some business leaders and wealthy individuals fund political campaigns to get legislation passed that will enable businesses to keep as much profit as possible at the expense of workers and customers. In each case, care has been taken to ensure that the population does not point the finger at the predatory practices of these wealthy entities but rather blame struggling Americans for their inability to achieve the American Dream.

Greed and fear has kept America from achieving its full potential. Unspeakable greed on the part of the elites and fear on the part of working-class Whites who worry another group could marginalize them. The idea that some working class Whites have been manipulated to hate others is not new. Legendary singer/songwriter Bob Dylan articulated this process in his song, "Only a Pawn in Their Game," which he wrote in response to the assassination of Civil Rights leader Medger Evers. Dylan performed the song during the 1963 March on Washington where Dr. Martin Luther King Jr. gave his iconic "I Have a Dream" speech. Regarding the killing of Evers and hatred of Blacks by "poor Whites," he advises us not to blame the poor White man because elite, wealthy Whites have manipulated him. As I will point out in the next chapter, this pattern of the elites manipulating the masses, which shockingly continues today, can be traced back to slavery—our nation's ugliest Black eye.

CHAPTER 3

From Slavery to Obama: The Black Experience

History, despite its wrenching pain,
cannot be unlived,
but if faced with courage,
need not be lived again.
—Maya Angelou

THE AFRICAN EXPERIENCE

The Creation of Race

Slavery is not unique to the U.S. The word "slave" was derived from the word "Slav." Slavs were prisoners of Slavonic tribes captured by Germans and sold to Arabs during the Middle Ages (Race timeline - go deeper, n.d.). The practice was a common aspect of life in Ancient Greece, Rome, and across the globe; however, it was typically based on religion, class, or a result of conquest, reasons having nothing to do with appearance.

Juan Garrido became the first known African to arrive in this country in 1513 during Juan Ponce de León's famous expedition to Florida in search of the Fountain of Youth (Gates, Jr., 2012). In 1619, the first

Africans to arrive in America were indentured servants, just as over 75% of the White colonists during that century (Takaki, 1993). The majority of immigrants were poor Whites trying to escape difficult economic conditions in England. Africans and poor Whites intermingled freely—they lived, worked, and played together. Class determined what life was like for these early Americans, with a small group of "planter elite" pulling the strings. Early on, given the difficult working conditions, most indentured workers did not survive long enough to fulfill their contracts. In the mid-17th century, a series of events would unfold that would establish the foundation for the problems with race that plague America today.

As economic conditions in England began to improve, fewer poor Whites were fleeing to America, resulting in a labor shortage. The dwindling supply of labor from England, coupled with the fact that indentured servants were beginning to live long enough to fulfill their contracts and, subsequently, demand land, caused desperation among the plantation owners. The system the owners had created to amass great riches was being threatened. The flashpoint occurred in 1676 after Black and White servants and slaves teamed up to attack the elite classes during Bacon's Rebellion. The planter elites then realized they needed a method of controlling the masses. The most convenient and sustainable solution to this problem was to create the world's first race-based slave system, particularly since the elites viewed Africans as stronger workers (Race timeline - go deeper, n.d.). To keep them under control and help them identify more with the plantation owners rather than their Black counterparts, the elites gave poor Whites new entitlements and employed them as overseers to control the slave population. Until this point, the most significant differences between people were with regard to religion. Early colonial laws had referred to people as Christians or Englishmen, but increasingly, the term "White" began to be used in legislation. Christians had been free, but to counteract the scores of Blacks who converted to Christianity, a Virginia court ruled that even Christians could be enslaved for life (Painter, 2006).

There is not enough space in this book to scratch the surface on the horrors of slavery, so I won't attempt to do so. A new generation of people gained a glimpse into the lives that millions of Americans endured as slaves by watching Alex Haley's groundbreaking mini-series *Roots*. I can remember watching this series as a young person and being very confused about why people like me were treated that way. I can remember feeling embarrassed, sad, and angry all at once. It is unfortunate that many of today's youth have no clue about some of the most significant events and practices in America's past. I asked a group of college students a few years ago if they had ever seen *Roots*. Not only had they not seen it, they didn't know what I was talking about.

Poor Whites were led to believe that a new system based on race was justified because of the natural inferiority of Blacks, specifically, but of any other nonwhite group as well. According to the PBS in their series, Race: the Power of an Illusion:

> Racial superiority was seen not only as 'natural' and inevitable but a moral responsibility for whites. The notions of Manifest Destiny and the White Man's Burden best capture this ideology of 'civilization' and racial difference (Race timeline - go deeper, n.d.).

Blacks began to be punished more harshly for crimes than their White counterparts, a practice that continues in some pockets of the legal system today. Blacks were routinely punished for wanting to improve themselves because it was believed that "learning will spoil the best nigger in the world" (Takaki, 1993, p. 123). Frederick Douglass, for instance, was severely beaten because he had learned to read and write as a slave. The planter elite knew that Blacks were not inferior. They denied opportunities for slaves to learn the language, customs, and traditions because they knew that they could and would learn them, which would prove that they were not inferior thinkers. In one of the most obvious instances of hypocrisy in American history, slavery persisted even as America fought for its independence from Great Britain during the American Revolution. When people dismiss slavery as just "the way things were," they minimize the fact that there were many people at the time who felt that the institution was wrong. For example, future First Lady Abigail Adams wrote in a letter to her husband John in 1765 regarding the hypocrisy of practicing slavery while fighting the Revolution, "How is it we are denying people that which we are fighting for ourselves" (Brunner, & Rowan, 2007)?

Racial Superiority and The Framers

Today, there is heated debate about how our revered Founding Fathers are depicted in history books. There were 70 delegates invited to the Constitutional Convention in 1787, of which 55 attended (National Archives, n.d.). We hold our framers in high esteem, and indeed we should because they were brilliant men with great vision and courage, and the document they created is remarkable. Many Americans seem to forget, however, that they were just men, not the mythical Gods we seem to make them out to be. People like to debate what the Framers' intended. There is no way that these men, even as intelligent and visionary as they were, could anticipate the Internet, artificial limbs, air travel, or 3D printing. The Constitution reflected the prevailing values and customs of the time and consequently, the hopes and dreams of the dominant culture—White men. Thankfully, these men were thoughtful enough to make the Constitution a living, flexible document.

Of the most prominent framers, 67% had owned slaves at some point (Iaccarino, n. d.). The fact that a nation founded on "equality" and "the natural rights of man" could simultaneously deny freedom to its Black residents is mind-boggling. The treatment of Blacks as less than full human beings is reflective of how strongly the South wanted to hold on to its system of free labor, and just how pervasive the view was that Blacks were inferior. It is hard for some people to accept that even though there were delegates who had already denounced slavery at the time of the Constitutional Convention and others who later did so, our nation was founded under a White supremacist ideology; the idea that Whites were inherently superior to Blacks. Declaration of Independence author, Thomas Jefferson, for instance, believed strongly in the superiority of Whites even though he thought slavery violated the natural rights of Blacks. Jefferson wrote in *Notes on the State of Virginia*, "I advance it therefore, as a suspicion only, that blacks [...] are inferior to the whites in the endowments of body and mind." Jefferson, by the way, owned over 200 slaves. His proposed solution to the problem of slavery, which gained some significant support, was to send Blacks back to Africa because they could never be assimilated. Again, it is convenient to excuse this behavior and sentiment as just the mentality of the time, but there were some forward thinking individuals even then who recognized slavery as an abomination and lobbied for complete equality for Blacks. What disturbs me about the Constitution Convention is the same thing that bothers me about politics today. Although there were people in the room who were adamantly opposed to slavery, they felt compelled to go along with the program to get Southern support for the document knowing that lives would be lost because of the deal.

The idea that Blacks were inferior helped to shape scientific research over subsequent decades. It was already widely accepted that Blacks were inferior, but scientists, such as Johann Blumenbach, were determined to prove as much. In 1776, Blumenbach developed a pyramid with five human types. He introduced the term Caucasian, based on a skull he found in the Caucasus Mountains that he described as having the "most beautiful form" (Brunner, & Rowen, 2007). He naturally placed Caucasian at the top of his pyramid. Samuel Morton, often referred to as America's first famous scientist reinforced Blumenbach's "findings" in 1839. Morton reported that the larger skulls of Caucasians gave them a "decided and unquestioned superiority over all the nations of the earth" (Brunner, & Rowen, 2007). Moreover, in 1854, scientist Josiah Nott claimed, "Nations and races, like individuals, have each an especial destiny: some are born to rule, and others to be ruled [...] No two distinctly marked races can dwell together on equal terms" (Brunner, & Rowen, 2007). Fortunately, subsequent scientists consistently deemed this early research on skull size between the races as "junk science."

Because of the widely accepted belief of Black inferiority and its associated economic windfalls, slavery flourished through the early to mid-1700s. Slavery was abolished in Massachusetts in 1783, and the Northwest Ordinance barred slavery from the Western territories in 1787, yet the 1790 Naturalization Act guaranteed that only Whites could be citizens. This idea was later challenged in 1857 with the Dred Scott case, but Blacks would not prevail (Painter, 2006). The U.S. Supreme Court Chief Justice Taney declared that Blacks have "no rights which any white man is bound to respect." Blacks were not guaranteed citizenship until nearly one hundred years later. Even in the North, Blacks were "free," but hardly living freely. Blacks were routinely discriminated against in various aspects of daily life and subjected to ridiculous penalties, such as being forced to pay bonds just to cross state borders. Many Blacks found themselves in urban areas (as they are still disproportionately located today), working under contracts where they had little negotiating power.

The Emancipation of Blacks

Between 1860 and 1861, eleven Southern states seceded over the issue of slavery, which ignited the Civil War. In 1863, the Emancipation Proclamation freed individuals enslaved in the Confederate-held territory. The Civil War didn't end until 1865, resulting in the ratification of the Thirteenth Amendment to the U.S. Constitution, which outlawed slavery in the entire nation. From 1865 to 1877, during the period of Reconstruction, Blacks experienced many significant social, political, and legal victories. They were aided by the presence of federal troops to keep them safe. Blacks opened businesses, held high-level elected positions, and began to acquire land. The Fourteenth Amendment was added to the U.S. Constitution in 1868 granting citizenship to freedmen. However, Southern states could continue to deprive Black citizens of equal rights because this amendment did not supersede federalism or "states rights" (Painter, 2006). The Fifteenth Amendment gave freedmen the conditional right to vote in 1870. In 1875, the Civil Rights Act was passed, prohibiting racial discrimination in hotels and other public accommodations. Reconstruction was a significant era in American history. While many Americans had long believed that Blacks were inferior and incapable of taking care of themselves and their communities, it was becoming obvious during this time that Blacks were well on their way to establishing themselves as full members of the American Community. The Southern States, spurred on by the wealthy elites, could not let that happen.

The Compromise of 1877 abruptly halted the progress of Blacks. Rutherford B. Hayes became president in a hotly disputed election only after agreeing to remove federal troops from the South, thus ending Reconstruction and abandoning Blacks to the politics of the Southern states (Painter, 2006). One can only imagine what things would be like for Black Americans today had Reconstruction been allowed to continue. Instead, all of the gains were lost. The 1875 Civil Rights Act was overturned in 1883. That year, the eugenics movement also began, which identified heredity as the cause of human behavioral and cultural differences. Veterans of the Confederate Army formed the Ku Klux Klan in Tennessee in 1886. The infamous Jim Crow era began in 1887. In 1896, in Plessy v. Ferguson, the U.S. Supreme Court declared segregation legal under the "separate but equal" formula, barring Blacks from Southern public life and civil rights (Painter, 2006). During this time, Blacks faced severe discrimination in education, housing, employment, public transportation, voting rights, and the criminal justice system— essentially every aspect of public and private life. Meanwhile, in 1899, the idea behind Manifest Destiny found a new mechanism—imperialism. The new targets were Puerto Rico, Guam, and the Philippines. Poet

Rudyard Kipling captured this thought process in his poem, *White Man's Burden*. In essence, Rudyard believed that since Whites were at the top of the human hierarchy, they naturally had a responsibility to govern inferior people (Brunner, & Rowen, 2007).

Out of options, Blacks began to flee the South from 1916 to 1919. The "Great Migration" saw over a half a million Black Southerners move to Northern cities in search of employment opportunities. Companies, eager to employ Blacks at a fraction of the rates they paid Whites, sponsored chartered buses to recruit workers. The manipulative practices of business owners prompted anti-Black riots in places like my birth home, East St. Louis, where Whites were the predominate but threatened labor force. Up to two hundred Blacks were killed and over six thousand Black people were left homeless as a result of the 1917 East St. Louis riot (Moore, 2013). There were so many violent riots across the country in the summer and fall of 1919 that it has been called "Red Summer," a reference to the widespread bloodshed (Wormser, n.d.). Red Summer proved disastrous for Blacks who had, despite blatant discrimination, built thriving communities, such as "Black Wall Street" in Tulsa and Rosewood, Florida, which was featured in the 1997 movie, *Rosewood*. The Tulsa riot resulted in approximately 10,000 Blacks being left homeless in what was the wealthiest Black community in America (Hirsch, 2002). These riots were started by Whites but frequently resulted in charges against Blacks.

By 1930, two million Blacks had migrated north with the promise of better lives (Takaki, 1993). Blacks still experienced segregation, racism, and housing and employment discrimination, particularly during the Great Depression, but seldom did they experience the violence they had known in the South. The "Great Migration," which continued into the 1930s during the Depression and accelerated in the 1940s, had a tremendous impact on the demographics of the country that can still be felt in today's segregated cities where large manufacturing companies once dominated the urban landscape (Leuchtenburg, n.d.).

The year 1936 marked a significant shift in American politics. Franklin D. Roosevelt was able to put together an unlikely political force, the "New Deal coalition," which consisted of union members and ethnic and religious minorities, as well as "the Solid South' (Leuchtenburg, n.d.). The shift by Blacks from the Republican to the Democratic party can still be felt today in American politics. The results of the shift in allegiances proved mixed for Blacks. On one hand, local authorities administered the New Deal's federal programs unevenly, favoring poor Whites over poor Blacks (Leuchtenburg, n.d.). Therefore, the initiative ultimately did little to improve the lives of Blacks relative to their White counterparts in terms of employment, wages, and working conditions (Painter, 2006). On the other hand, federal help had been virtually non-existent in the South prior to the programs introduced through the New Deal (Leuchtenburg, n.d.). Most significantly, Blacks felt that they had a voice and a federal government that at least considered their needs.

America's Biggest Missed Opportunity

Post-WWII may have been the best chance for America to right the wrongs of slavery. Under the G.I. Bill, the federal government created programs to subsidize affordable loans for millions of Americans to buy homes and go to college. For many, this period marked a significant shift in the lives of their families for generations to come. Many White recipients were the first in their families to go to college or own a home, which represented wealth. Unfortunately, while Blacks qualified for the programs in theory, they could not take advantage of them in practice. The government introduced a national appraisal system, "redlining," that resulted in "for Whites only" suburbs and Black dominated inner-cities. The significance of this era cannot be overstated. Black veterans, despite their individual merit or work ethic, could not purchase homes in upscale neighborhoods. It is no coincidence that Blacks make up the population in and around urban areas in America today. Not only were the White veterans able to buy homes, their newly acquired homes could later be mortgaged for the education of their children and grandchildren. Those homes have also been used to transfer wealth, of which some of those families are still enjoying. In fact, estimates are as much as 80% of lifetime wealth is accumulated through intergenerational transfers ("Background readings," n.d.). Not only was housing an issue, there were problems for Black veterans on the education side of the equation as well. Predominately White colleges and universities offered few opportunities to Blacks strictly because of their race, so many enrolled in Historically Black Colleges and Universities (HBCU's). Unfortunately, many people were wait-listed because there were not enough HBCU's to meet the demand. These are really significant facts that have gotten very little attention in today's discussions about hard work and merit. Many Americans admittedly identify the G.I. Bill as the instrument that forever changed the fate of their families, yet they seem unaware of the restrictions that barred Blacks from experiencing the same boost. Ironically, some of these same people are the most vocal against government programs designed to aid people in need.

Other legislation worked against Blacks during that time. For instance, in 1935 Congress passed the Social Security Act, which exempted agricultural workers and domestic servants, who were predominantly Black, Mexican, and Asian, from receiving old-age insurance. That same year Congress passed the Wagner Act, which guaranteed workers' rights but did not prohibit unions from racial discrimination. When people remark that Blacks should be doing better in America because slavery has been over for a long time, they are either unaware of or dismissive of the affect of these key policies and practices.

Continuation of Jim Crow

In 1948, the Democratic Party's nominating convention adopted a strong civil rights slate resulting in Southern delegates walking out and forming the States' Rights or "Dixiecrat" party (Painter, 2006). For Blacks in the South, life was not only difficult but also dangerous. Between 1877 and 1950, nearly 4,000 black men, women, and children were lynched in the South (Lynching in America, n.d.). The "Montgomery bus boycotts" of 1955 and 1956 led to the passage of the Civil Rights Act of 1957, but conditions were still not acceptable for Blacks. Jim Crow laws made life hardly tolerable. "For Whites only" signs harkened back to many of the Founding Fathers' perception that Blacks were inferior to Whites. Imagine adults having to be subservient to not only White adults, but to White kids as well. Think about what that did to the psyche of Black people in general, and Black men in particular. Jim Crow would make life difficult for Blacks until the Civil Rights Movement prompted President Lyndon Johnson to sign the Civil Rights Act of 1964 and the Voting Rights Act of 1965, landmark legislation finally representing a real shot at the American Dream for Black Americans.

Racial Code Words

Some people trace today's vitriolic political climate regarding race relations back to Ronald Reagan's time as President. Every election cycle, numerous politicians conjure the name Reagan as many times as they can on the campaign trail despite the negative perception of his presidency shared by many Blacks. In 1980, Reagan was elected president of the United States advocating "states' rights" and promising to end Affirmative Action. He, despite Black people's objections, kicked off his campaign in Philadelphia, Mississippi, where three civil rights workers had been brutally murdered in 1964. Reagan was well aware of the tensions that existed when he visited, particularly since nobody was convicted of the murders until 2005. (Dewan, 2005). Bob Herbert wrote in a New York Times Op Ed:

> Everybody watching the 1980 campaign knew what Reagan was signaling at the fair. Whites and blacks, Democrats and

Republicans—they all knew. The news media knew. The race haters and the people appalled by racial hatred knew. And Reagan knew. He was tapping out the code. It was understood that when politicians started chirping about "states' rights" to white people in places like Neshoba County, they were saying that when it comes down to you and the blacks, we're with you (2007).

The following statement might illicit an emotional reaction from you that might make you put down this book, but I think it is important for people to know how deep the disdain for Reagan was in poor, Black communities like East St. Louis. I can remember coming home from school on the day that Reagan was shot to see people dancing and cheering. While that is certainly not an appropriate response to the President being shot, if you understand the fragility of the human mind, you can understand why people felt that way. For many Black Americans, Reagan's philosophies stood for marginalization and isolation. History seems to have forgotten that (1) he opposed the Civil Rights Act of 1964; (2) he tried to weaken the Voting Rights Act of 1965 after he became president; (3) he was against having a national holiday for Dr. Martin Luther King, Jr.'s birthday; (4) he vetoed a bill to expand federal Civil Rights legislation— a veto which Congress overrode; and (5) he vetoed a bill that would impose sanctions on South Africa during Apartheid—a veto which Congress also overrode (Herbert, B., 2007). Moreover, Republican operative Lee Atwater, a close advisor to Reagan, later admitted what many Blacks had always suspected. In a 1981 interview, believing that he would not be quoted, Atwater explains the use of these code words:

"You start out in 1954 by saying, 'Nigger, nigger, nigger.' By 1968 you can't say 'nigger'—that hurts you, backfires. So you say stuff like, uh, forced busing, states' rights, and all that stuff, and you're getting so abstract. Now, you're talking about cutting taxes, and all these things you're talking about are totally economic things and a byproduct of them is, blacks get hurt worse than whites [...] 'We want to cut this,' is much more abstract than even the busing thing, uh, and a hell of a lot more abstract than 'Nigger, nigger' (Perlstein, n.d.).

Every time today's politicians refer to Reagan as their hero—America's hero, or use the same code words that Atwater acknowledged were used only to gain support of Southern racists, in other words "playing the race card," it makes many Blacks feel as though their lives still don't matter. For many Blacks, the mere name Ronald Reagan has become one of those code words.

Twenty-First Century Challenges

There are people who are steadfastly opposed to Affirmative Action (AA). Opponents will tell you that because of such programs, Blacks are taking all the jobs. With the Black unemployment rate being so high, the obvious question is, "If Blacks are taking all of the jobs, what are they doing with them because they sure aren't keeping them?" Critics believe AA is unfair and results in "reverse discrimination." First, it is important to point out that there is no such thing as "reverse discrimination." Discrimination against Whites is called "discrimination," just as is discrimination against Blacks. Additionally, the problems with programs such as AA are often in the failed implementation by people who don't believe in the programs in the first place. In other words, if I hire the first Black applicant I meet regardless of qualifications only to fill a quota, my approach will backfire on the applicant and the organization. On the other hand, if I understand that my hiring past practices have unfairly resulted in adverse outcomes for Blacks, I become more proactive in seeking out qualified Blacks candidates, I am more likely to find a win-win scenario.

The results of such programs have been mixed. Thousands of qualified individuals who might have been overlooked in the past have been employed through these programs. Because of some opportunities were able to take advantage of, many Black children are more likely to go to college and attain a promising career. Directly or indirectly as a result of a more proactive approach to being inclusive, there have been shining examples of successes that were thought impossible just a couple of decades ago, such as having a mixed race person ascend to the highest office in the land. Blacks, however, still experience poorer quality of life outcomes compared to their White counterparts. Here is just a snapshot of Black life in the U.S.:

EDUCATION

- In 2012, the dropout rate for Whites was 4 percent compared to 8 percent for Blacks.

- By 2013, the percentage of Whites between 25 and 29 years of age who had attained a bachelor's or higher degree was 40% and 20% for Blacks. For master's degrees it was 9 percent to 3 percent, respectively (Kena, Aud, Johnson, Wang, Zhang, Rathbun, Wilkinson-Flicker, & Kristapovich, 2014).

- Black students were more than four times as likely to attend schools where fewer than 60% of teachers meet all state certification and licensure requirements ("Data Collection: Data Snapshot - Teacher Equity," 2014).

EMPLOYMENT

- The unemployment rate for Blacks (10.4%) is more than double the rate for Whites (4.7 percent) ("Employment status of the civilian population by race, sex, and age," n.d.). At every level of educational attainment, Whites have a lower unemployment rate than Blacks.

- There are only five Fortune 500 African America CEO's (African American chairman & CEO's of Fortune 500 companies, 2015).

- Black-owned businesses only make up 7 percent of all U.S firms and less than one half of 1 percent of all U.S business receipts (United States Census Bureau, 2011).

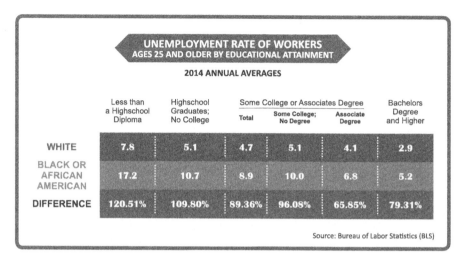

UNEMPLOYMENT RATE OF WORKERS
AGES 25 AND OLDER BY EDUCATIONAL ATTAINMENT

2014 ANNUAL AVERAGES

	Less than a Highschool Diploma	Highschool Graduates; No College	Some College or Associates Degree			Bachelors Degree and Higher
			Total	Some College; No Degree	Associate Degree	
WHITE	7.8	5.1	4.7	5.1	4.1	2.9
BLACK OR AFRICAN AMERICAN	17.2	10.7	8.9	10.0	6.8	5.2
DIFFERENCE	120.51%	109.80%	89.36%	96.08%	65.85%	79.31%

Source: Bureau of Labor Statistics (BLS)

INCOME

- Blacks earn less than Whites at each level of education from not graduating high school through terminal degree (Bureau of Labor Statistics, n.d.).

- As of 2010, White families earned about $2 for every $1 that black and Hispanic families earned, a ratio that has remained roughly constant for the last 30 years (Lowrey, 2013).

MEDIAN USUAL WEEKLY EARNINGS OF FULL-TIME WAGE AND SALARY WORKERS
AGES 25 AND OLDER BY EDUCATIONAL ATTAINMENT

2014 ANNUAL AVERAGES

	Less than a Highschool Diploma	Highschool Graduates; No College	Some College or Associates Degree	Bachelors Degree Only	Bachelors Degree and Higher	Advanced Degree
WHITE	493	696	791	1,132	1,219	1,390
BLACK OR AFRICAN AMERICAN	440	579	637	895	970	1,149
DIFFERENCE	-10.75%	-16.81%	-19.47%	-20.95%	-20.43%	-17.34%

Source: Bureau of Labor Statistics (BLS)

- In 2013, the real median household income for Blacks was $34,598 compared to $58,270 for Whites (DeNavas-Walt, & Proctor, 2014).

WEALTH

- The share of wealth that Blacks hold continues to stand at a pedestrian rate. At the end of slavery, Blacks held .05 percent of the nations wealth, today that figure is only about 1 percent (Background readings, n.d.).
- The Great Recession has had a disproportionate effect on Blacks, including a doubling of the wealth gap between Whites and Blacks. By 2010, the average White family had about $632,000 in wealth, versus $98,000 for Black families (Lowrey, 2013).
- The wealth of White households was 13 times the median wealth of Black households in 2013 (Kochhar, & Fry, 2014).

INCARCERATION

- Blacks now constitute nearly 1 million of the total 2.3 million incarcerated population.
- Whites comprise 53% of the juvenile population, but only 33% of incarcerated youth. Black youth are 14% of all youth, but 40% of incarcerated youth (Rovner, 2014).
- Black males have a 32% chance of serving time in prison at some point in their lives compared to a 6 percent chance for White males ("Facts about prisons and people in prisons," 2014).

HEALTH

- The preterm birth rate for Black infants (17.1%) was approximately 60% higher than that for White infants (10.8%). The infant mortality rate for Blacks was more than double that for Whites in 2008 (CDC, 2013).
- The rates of premature death from stroke and coronary heart disease were higher among Blacks than Whites (CDC, 2013).

- During 1999-2008, both life expectancy and expected years of life free of activity limitations caused by chronic conditions were significantly greater for Whites than for Blacks (CDC, 2013).

HOUSING

- Blacks are 79% more likely than Whites to live in neighborhoods with industrial pollution (Roake, 2010).

- The percentage of the Black population is over twice as large in urban food deserts than in other urban areas (Dutko, Van Ploeg, & Farrigan, 2012).

- Forty-eight percent of public housing households are Black compared to only 19% of all renter households that are Black (United States Department of Housing and Urban Development, Office of Policy Development and Research. n.d.).

These statistics only tell part of the story. People of color continue to experience racism at individual, institutional, and structural levels in America. Individual racism is the bigotry, bias, and prejudice that individual exhibit. By institutional racism, I am referring to biased organizational policies, practices, and procedures. Structural racism is defined as, "A system in which public policies, institutional practices, cultural representations, and other norms work in various, often reinforcing ways to perpetuate racial group inequity" (Lawrence, Sutton, Kubisch, Susi, & Fulbright-Anderson, p. 11, 2004). Individual racism leads to institutional racism and institutional racism feeds structural racism.

SUMMARY

There is much discourse in America today about why Blacks continue to struggle while other groups have seemingly overcome their early mistreatment in America. In the case of the Irish and Jews, their skin color provided them the opportunity to blend in by just changing their names. Additionally, the right to vote led to political and, subsequently, economic power as they began to elect people who were like them. Many Asian groups have sent their best and brightest to live in America, so it's no miracle that they are able to overcome hurdles that average people could not. The Black experience has been unique. The level of disdain that some Whites have for Blacks is palpable, which is partially reflected in hate crime statistics. Moreover, the subtle and obvious conditioning of Blacks and Whites has worked to a significant degree. What many people don't take into account is the long-term cumulative effect of the different forms of racism, both in terms of the discriminatory practices that result from racist thinking, and also from the psychological and emotional toll this has taken on its victims. After all, as pointed out in the figure below, 83% of the Black experience has been dominated by slavery and other legal discrimination; the remaining 17% has been dominated by varying levels of individual, institutional, and structural bias or discrimination.

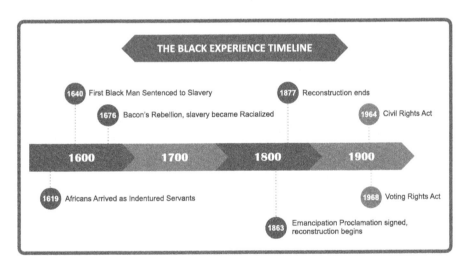

People tend to react more to symptoms as opposed to the root causes that undergird the issues. For too many Whites, racial disparities serve as indicators that Blacks really do not have what it takes, or they are too lazy to try. For too many Blacks, these numbers serve as indicators that either they really do not stack up, or the country does not want them to succeed, so tens of thousands of little Black kids ask themselves, "Why try?" In other words, the vulnerable human mind has led to conscious and subconscious actions by White elites to maintain their social, political, and economic dominance, as well as conscious and subconscious actions by people of color to perpetuate their subordinate status in America. And it is no accident!

As illustrated below, it is this lethal mix that thwarts the individual and collective growth of America. The Predatory Elite, the group that benefits most from the status quo, uses their influence to (1) establish conditions that result in education and economic barriers for Blacks and working

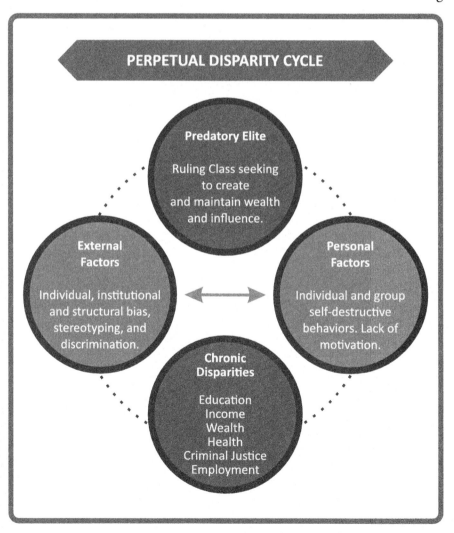

class Whites (External Factors); (2) Blacks react to these barriers with destructive anger, unproductive fear, or debilitating hopelessness (Personal Factors); (3) negative Personal Factors lead to additional debilitating External Factors; (4) the result is perpetual Chronic Disparities; and (5) the Chronic Disparities result in the Predatory Elite gaining more influence.

PART II

PERPETUATING THE DISPARITIES: DANCING TO OUR DOOM

CHAPTER 4

The Fix is In: From Outright Discrimination to Hidden Bias

If we accept and acquiesce in the face of discrimination,
we accept the responsibility ourselves.
We should, therefore, protest openly everything . . .
that smacks of discrimination or slander.
—Mary McLeod Bethune

WHY BLACKS CAN'T GET OVER IT

Simply put, Blacks can't get over it because it is not over. The disparities I pointed out in Chapter 3 are well documented, if not well known. To say that each of them is 100% a direct result of racism would be a stretch, but to deny racism is a significant factor is problematic. I have already cited FBI hate group and hate crime statistics, which are indisputably influenced by race. I have laid out a short history of America's experience with immigrants and provided some insight into slavery, which was undeniably about race. Moreover, I went into great detail of the harrowing experience of Blacks in the Jim Crow era, which was openly about race. This unapologetic discrimination was not that long ago. Some of the people who committed some of the worst atrocities during that time may still be alive. Unless they have had a personal metamorphosis, they probably hold firm to their opinions of Blacks, and they have undoubtedly shared those thoughts and feelings with their kids and grandkids who, in turn, may have shared those thoughts with their kids. Lingering beliefs about superiority and inferiority coupled with common "hidden" biases have resulted in continued widespread discrimination against Blacks.

The statistics that I outlined in Chapter 3 demonstrate numerous factors that lead to the disparities Blacks are experiencing in key areas of life in America. The items below describe actual discrimination that Blacks have experienced over recent years in those same key areas of life. Keep in mind that these experiences have nothing at all to do with Black Americans' individual merit, but rather their group affiliation—having Black skin.

EDUCATION

- Black students represent only 18% of total preschool enrollment, but 42% of students suspended (US Dept. of Education, 2014). Black boys, in particular, were more likely to be suspended for the same behavior that White boys weren't.

- After college preparatory students evaluated CVs of professors of different races on measures of competence, legitimacy, and interpersonal skills, Black professors were evaluated to be significantly less competent than their White and Asian counterparts regardless of actual background, training, and experience (Bavishi, Madera, & Hebl, 2010).

- In a study exploring how law firms would rate a hypothetical memo from a law student, Thomas Meyer, some firms were told the student was Black and some firms were told the student was White. The same memo received an average score of 3.2 for the Black Thomas Meyer and 4.1 for the White Thomas Meyer. Double the amount of spelling and grammar errors were found, more technical writing errors were found, and more errors of fact were found in the Black Thomas Meyer's memo (Reeves, 2014).

EMPLOYMENT

- In a study conducted by Devah Pager at Princeton, White applicants were more than twice as likely to receive a callback relative to equally qualified Black applicants. Whites with a felony conviction fared just as well if not better, than Black applicants with a clean background (Devah, 2008).

- A team of professors from MIT and the University of Chicago submitted 5,000 resumes, categorized into what they called White-sounding names and Black-sounding names, to 1,250 actual job postings (Bertrand, & Mullainathan, 2004). The researchers used birth records to categorize the names as White-sounding or Black-sounding. They were surprised to learn that Brendan, Gregg, Emily, and Anne received 50% more responses than Tamika, Aisha, Rasheed, and Tyrone. Having a White-sounding name mattered more than work ethic, experience, or any other merit-based criteria in the study. Even more troubling, a resume with a Black-sounding name with education listed from a prestigious university was no more likely to generate a callback than one with a Black-sounding name from a much less renowned institution, but the opposite was true for the resumes with White-sounding names. More prestige meant more callbacks for Whites. In other words, a Black person from Harvard was still a "just a Black person" to the perspective employers.

- The 2013 unemployment rate for recent college grads who are Black was almost twice that of recent college grads overall (Berman, 2014).

INCOME

- At every level of education, Blacks earn less than their White counterparts (Bureau of Labor Statistics, n.d.).

- In 2011, researchers found that a $10,000 increase in the average annual income of an occupation translated into a 7 percent drop in the share of Black men doing that job (Berman, 2014).

- In a study exploring tipping behavior and race, both White and Black restaurant customers tipped Black servers less than their White coworkers, regardless of the performance of the server (Brewster, & Lynn, 2014).

INCARCERATION

- In 2002, Blacks constituted more than 80% of the people sentenced under the federal crack cocaine laws and served substantially more time in prison for drug offenses than did Whites, despite that fact that more than two-thirds of crack cocaine users in the U.S. are White or Hispanic.

- Blacks represent only 12% of the total population of drug users, but 38% of all people arrested for drug offenses, and 59% of all people in state prison for a drug offense. Moreover, Blacks serve virtually as much time in prison for a drug offense (58.7 months) as Whites do for a violent offense (61.7 months) (National Association for the Advancement of Colored People, n.d.).

- Among adolescents aged 12 to 17 admitted to substance abuse treatment nationwide, Blacks were significantly more likely than Whites to be involved with the criminal justice system, even after controlling for actual criminal behaviors, substance abuse, mental health problems, and socio-environmental risk (Godette, Mulatu, Leonard, Randolph, Williams, 2011). In other words, Whites are offered the opportunity to seek treatment for these issues without being treated as criminals.

HEALTH

- Physicians were 23% more verbally dominant and engaged in 33% less patient-centered communication with Black patients than with White patients (Johnson, Roter, Powe, & Cooper, 2004).

- Race and insurance are strong predictors of discharge to rehabilitation among adult traumatic brain injury (TBI) survivors in the United States. Blacks are not afforded the opportunities that their White counterparts have in terms of access to rehabilitation after TBI (Asemota, George, Cumpsty-Fowler, Haider, & Schneider, 2013).

- Doctors were much less likely to recommend cardiac catheterization, a helpful procedure, to Black patients—even when their medical files were statistically identical to those of White patients (Mullainathan, 2015).

HOUSING

- A study published by the National Bureau of Economic Research analyzes more than two million sale prices from 1990 to 2008 for equivalent homes in the same neighborhoods purchased by White, Black, and Hispanic buyers. Researchers concentrate on neighborhoods in Chicago, Baltimore/Washington, D.C., San Francisco, and Los Angeles (Duke Social Sciences Research Institute, 2014). On average, that Black and Hispanic buyers paid 3 to 4 percent more on equivalent homes than their White counterparts.

- In the run-up to the Great Recession, Black borrowers were more frequently offered high-interest, sub-prime mortgages than their White counterparts, even when they qualified for better terms (Bouie, 2014). In a study of peer-to-peer lending, researchers found that Blacks were 25% to 35% less likely to receive funding than their White counterparts with similar credit (Chen, 2012).

- Black renters who contact agents about recently advertised housing units learn about 11% fewer available units and are shown roughly 4 percent fewer units. Black homebuyers who contact agents about recently advertised homes for sale learn about 17% fewer available homes and are shown about 18% fewer homes (Gonzalez, 2013).

The ABC News special, *True Colors*, highlighted America's continuing racial challenges. The hidden cameras followed two friends, one Black and one White, as they completed all the activities that one would need to do when relocating—buying a vehicle, finding a place to live, and getting a job. Consistently, the White person was welcomed while the Black person was discouraged. The Black person was charged higher prices, misled about job openings, and lied to about housing availability (True Colors Product Overview, 2008). ABC has conducted a subsequent set of hidden camera studies in their series *What Would You Do?*, where they staged a number of these experiments to capture what everyday people would do in uncomfortable situations. The researchers found that White people were consistently given better treatment. One of the scenarios involved two actors sitting in a park pretending to be distraught. The news crew wanted to determine what percentage of passersby would stop to help. The White actor was helped more than three times as often as the Black actor (Berman, 2008). In staged fighting between interracial couples, race influenced who intervened and with which couples (Taylor & Jaquez, 2008). None of this prepared me for what ABC captured in a scenario where they instructed three White teen actors to vandalize a car in an upscale, predominately White neighborhood (Taylor & Jaquez, 2008). The kids drew a great deal of attention, but the reaction was completely different when ABC replaced the three boys with Black actors. People were outraged at the behavior they observed. Several witnesses confronted the teens or called the police. What surprised the producers the most, however, was the number of phone calls that the police received from Whites concerned about several Black teens sleeping in a car in the parking lot around the corner from the staged scenario. The sleeping boys were relatives of the Black actors who had given them a ride to the set. The callers said they looked suspicious, but the cameras showed them innocently napping while waiting for the actors to finish the scene. Black teens sleeping in a car drew more ire from Whites than White kids vandalizing a car in broad daylight.

Americans are woefully ineffective at dealing with the complexities that have resulted in the statistics and behaviors I have outlined. Clearly, something terribly wrong is happening. I am not convinced that the studies I have cited or scenarios from ABC are proof of racial hatred. While there are still people who hate others merely based on race, I believe that the overwhelming majority of people are past that point. I think most Americans try to do the right thing. How, then, can these issues continue to pop-up? I believe the answer can be found only through a more sophisticated understanding of the human brain.

NATURE'S BRILLIANT, YET VULNERABLE MACHINE

I have been hearing all my life from the United Negro College Fund, that "a mind is a terrible thing to waste." Their famous advertising campaign began in 1972, the year that I was born. Regarding America's challenge to achieve racial harmony, we are doing just that—wasting our minds' capacity to figure this out. Part of the problem is that we learn so little about how this complex machine works. Really, how often do you think about thinking? For us to virtually ignore all that scientists have learned about the brain—how it is developed, how it operates, how it can be fractured, and how it can be strengthened—is profoundly irresponsible. Even worse is the fact that experts, the people on whom we rely to teach us about who we are, have not to a significant degree connected the dots to apply their findings from other contexts to solve challenges with race relations. Understanding the human brain's strengths and vulnerabilities helps to explain how issues related to race developed in the first place and, more importantly, why they persist.

About the Brain

Human beings have over 100 billion neurons. Each of us can store the equivalent of 10 million books of over 1,000 pages in our heads (Howard, 2006). Our brains can absorb two million bytes of information per second (Carson & Lewis, 2000). What the average person can do is remarkable, but what some of us can do is stunning. Imagine memorizing 3.14159265358979323846264338327950288419716939937510582 0974944592307816406286208998628034825342117067. That is Pi to 100 digits. Daniel Tammet has memorized Pi to 22,514 digits. He can also speak English, French, Finnish, German, Spanish, Lithuanian, Romanian, Estonian, Icelandic, Welsh, and Esperanto (Tammet, 2006). Tammet has an extremely rare case of Asperger's called Savant Syndrome. Even rarer is the fact the Tammet is highly functioning in daily life and can verbalize his experiences. Savants typically struggle with negotiating daily life and have less developed social skills, as demonstrated by Dustin Hoffman's critically acclaimed portrayal of an autistic savant in the film *Rain Man (Treffert, n.d.).* How can an individual's brain be capable of such brilliance in music, art, mathematics, and mechanical or spatial skills, yet struggle with activities average people do each day? While there is a lot yet to learn, our understanding of this incredible machine becomes more sophisticated each day.

We know that there are three interconnected layers in the brain: (1) the central core, which is comprised of the thalamus, pons, cerebellum, reticular formation, and medulla; (2) the limbic system, comprised of the hippocampus, amygdala, and hypothalamus; and (3) the cerebral cortex, comprised of the frontal lobe, occipital lobe, parietal lobe, and temporal lobe. The central core, found in all vertebrates, helps to regulate essential life processes like breathing, sleep, and movement. The limbic system, which exists only in mammals, regulates processes like body temperature and blood pressure, as well as motivation, emotions, and memory. I have written more about this system later in the book. The cerebral cortex contains two hemispheres, left and right. It has long been believed that the left hemisphere, often referred to as the "left brain," is where language, logic, interpretation, and arithmetic are thought to live. The right hemisphere, often referred to as the "right brain," is where the ability to do geometry, nonverbal processes, visual pattern recognition, auditory skills, and spatial skills are believed to live. However, there is reason to be skeptical about the left brain/right brain divide. New research, including that of Stephen M. Kosslyn and G. Wayne Miller, suggests that contrary to popular belief, "the sweeping characterizations of the two halves of the brain miss the mark: one is not logical and the other intuitive, one analytical and the other creative" (2013). They suggest that the unique functioning of the left and right halves of the brain are wildly exaggerated. The popular theory suggests that people are either "left brain" or "right brain" dominated. On the contrary, these systems work simultaneously in each of us to make us "intelligent" beings. Clearly, intelligent beings ought to be able to overcome our issues with race, correct? Maybe we are not as intelligent as we think.

Rethinking Intelligence

What really is intelligence and how is it measured? The Binet-Simon Intelligence Test was introduced in 1905 as the first practical test of intelligence. After several revisions in 1916, the test became known as the Stanford–Binet Intelligence Scale, which became the most widely used test in the United States. Early research in the field of intelligence focused on the *g*, or general factor, which was thought to be the primary mental ability that all existing intelligence tests had in common (Binet & Simon, 1916; Carroll, 1997; Gardner, 1998; Keith, 1994; Sternberg, 2000; & Wechsler, 1958). Thorndike (1920) divided intelligent activity into three types: social intelligence, concrete intelligence, and abstract intelligence. David Wechsler argued that non-intellective aspects of general intelligence be included with any measure of complete intelligence (Wechsler, 1958). His Weschler Adult Intelligence Scale (WAIS), developed in 1939, overtook the Stanford-Binet Test in popularity. Wechsler's series of tests are still the most widely administered IQ tests in the world? (Kaplan, & Saccuzzo, 2009).

While the most accepted measure of intelligence remains IQ, its significance is debatable. Researchers indicate that IQ might account for less than 10% of real-world success (Akers & Porter, 2003; Cooper & Sawaf, 1997; Stein & Book, 2000). So what about the other 90%? In the 1980s, Howard Gardner gained much acclaim for his theory of multiple intelligences (MI) (Gardner, 1983). Gardner has identified eight different types of intelligence: linguistic, logic-mathematical, musical, spatial, bodily/kinesthetic, interpersonal, intrapersonal, and naturalistic (Gardner, 2011). His theory has been criticized for a lack of empirical evidence but remains popular, particularly with educators. One of the reasons that Gardner's theory appeals to many people because we intuitively sense that there is something more important than IQ. Each of us can name a person we know who has tremendous raw intelligence but struggles with what we might think of as common-sense aspects of life. Even Albert Einstein was careful about focusing too much on IQ. He warned us that "We should take care not to make the intellect our God; it has, of course, powerful muscles, but no personality. It cannot lead, it can only serve; and it is not fastidious in its choices of a leader" (Einstein, 1996).

I think of emotional intelligence as the personality to which Einstein referred. Dr. Peter Salovey of Yale and Dr. John Mayer of the University of New Hampshire are credited with coining the term "emotional intelligence" in 1990, but it was the crossover appeal of Daniel Goleman that took the subject from academic circles to business circles. There has been an explosion of interest in EI since the 1985 release of Goleman's long-running New York Times Best Seller, *Emotional Intelligence* (e.g., Bar-On & Parker, 2000; Bar-On, Tranel, Denburg, & Bechara, 2003; Caruso, Mayer, & Salovey, 2002; Cherniss, 2002; Goleman, 1995; 1998; 2005; Mayer, Caruso, & Salovey, 1999; Mayer, Salovey, & Caruso,

2000; Salovey & Sluyter, 1997; Salovey & Mayer, 1990). Regarding the high efficacy of EI, Goleman wrote, "Analyses done by dozens of different experts in close to 500 corporations, governmental agencies, and nonprofit organizations worldwide have arrived independently at remarkably similar conclusions" (1995, p. 5). According to Cooper and Sawaf (1997), "Modern science is proving every day that it is EI, not IQ or raw brain power alone that underpins the best decisions, the most dynamic organizations, and the most satisfying and successful lives" (p. xii). Traditional IQ can be regarded as a threshold factor, in other words, one needs a certain amount of IQ to do a particular job, but additional IQ points won't likely affect one's performance. Improving one's EI will, however, affect performance. According to Simmons and Simmons (1997), while areas such as "technical skills, specific knowledge, mental abilities, physical fitness, physical appearance, interest in a particular type of work, aspirations and career goals, and life circumstances" also affect what a person accomplishes in life, EI might matter the most (p. 12). IQ and EI are not highly correlated, so the two are not at odds. Think of EI as helping to get the most out of a given IQ level. Dr. Ruven Bar-On, who developed the first commercially available instrument to measure EI, the EQ-i (now EQi 2.0), noted that, "EI combines with other important determinants, such as biomedical predispositions and conditions, cognitive intellectual capacity, as well as the reality and limitations of the immediate and ever-changing environment" to produce high performance (Bar-On, 1997, p. 14).

While there are various definitions of EI, it is essentially defined as successfully recognizing and managing one's emotions while effectively recognizing and responding to the emotions of others (Bar-On, 1997; Goleman, 1995; 1998; Mayer & Salovey, 1995). Dr. Bar-On considers these to be the criteria for EI:

(a) the ability to recognize, understand, and express emotions and feelings

(b) the ability to understand how others feel and relate with them

(c) the ability to manage and control emotions

(d) the ability to manage change, adapt, and solve problems of a personal and interpersonal nature

(e) the ability to generate positive affect and be self-motivated.

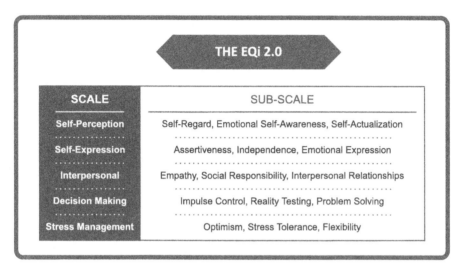

THE EQi 2.0	
SCALE	SUB-SCALE
Self-Perception	Self-Regard, Emotional Self-Awareness, Self-Actualization
Self-Expression	Assertiveness, Independence, Emotional Expression
Interpersonal	Empathy, Social Responsibility, Interpersonal Relationships
Decision Making	Impulse Control, Reality Testing, Problem Solving
Stress Management	Optimism, Stress Tolerance, Flexibility

Despite the typical connotation regarding emotion, EI is not "touchy-feely" stuff. This is neuroscience! There are many theories about how the brain processes emotions. One way to think about how the brain processes is: (a) a situation presents itself, (b) emotional impulses go from the amygdala to the prefrontal cortex of the brain, (c) the prefrontal cortex receives and analyzes the information and then decides the appropriate response (Goleman, Boyatzis, & McKee, 2002, p. 28). Emotions are more powerful than intellect in critical times because, "As our radar for emotional emergencies, the amygdala can commandeer other parts of the brain, including rational centers in the neocortex, for immediate action if it perceives a threat" (Goleman, Boyatzis, & McKee, 2002, p. 28). A popular metaphor for how this process works describes a "high road" or "low road." Under this theory, the "low road" represents a direct pathway from the thalamus to the amygdala for fear responses, which bypasses conscious processing so that people can respond immediately to fearful stimuli (LeDoux, 1996). An alternate "high road," pathway routes the incoming information through the sensory cortex, which enables it to be consciously processed and integrated with higher-level cognitive processes (LeDoux, 1996). However, new research has emerged that challenges this metaphor. According to Luiz Pessoa and Ralph Adolphs in Nature Revies Neuroscience, "Ultimately, the fate of a biologically-relevant stimulus should not be understood in terms of a 'low road' versus a 'high road', but in terms of the 'multiple roads' that lead to the expression of observed behaviors" (2010). In other words, the process is more complex than first believed. What experts do agree on is the importance of emotion in our daily lives.

When the brain does not process emotions effectively, we are lost. For example, Damasio (1994) wrote about an individual with above average intelligence who suffered damage to part of his brain associated with emotional experience. While this patient's IQ was still intact after the damage as indicated by high scores on cognitive tests and the ability to solve complex problems, simple daily tasks became impossible to manage without the capacity to experience emotions. His interpersonal relationships were strained because of his inability to feel and demonstrate his own emotions or understand and appreciate the emotional mood of others. The patient eventually lost his wife and his job. In another study of neurological patients selected from the patient registry of the University of Iowa's Division of Cognitive Neuroscience, Bar-On, Tranel, Denberg, and Bechara (2003) provide empirical evidence in support of the hypothesis that EI is different from and more effective than cognitive intelligence. Patients significantly low in EI were found to experience poor judgment in decision-making and disturbances in social functioning in spite of normal levels of cognitive intelligence.

Emotional Intelligence and Diversity

When I came across Goleman's seminal book early in my career, I was hooked. The connection was deeply personal for me. I was immediately convinced that EI was partly responsible for helping me make it out of East St. Louis. I had known many intelligent folks for whom success eluded, so I understood that IQ or raw intelligence could only take one so far. I decided to take the EQi assessment and my scores were above average. I was so impressed by what I had read and experienced, that I later decided to focus my business on keynote speaking, training, coaching, and consulting on EI. Over the past decade, I have reached thousands with education and training on EI to help them make a more positive impact at work and at home.

I have been particularly interested in how EI affects one's understanding and appreciation of diversity, beginning with my doctoral dissertation study, *The Relationship Between Emotional Intelligence and Intercultural Sensitivity* (Conrad, 2006). It seemed obvious to me that characteristics such as empathy, social responsibility, and interpersonal relationships would be highly correlated with one's ability to connect with people across diverse experiences. What I found using the EQi along with the Intercultural Development Inventory (IDI). "Problem Solving," the least "soft" sounding sub-scale of the EQi, ended up being the most highly correlated sub-scale with the total score on the IDI.

The reason I find this surprising is that I do an exercise with groups where I ask individuals to guess which sub-scale mattered the most in my study. Rarely, if ever, do they pick Problem Solving. I believe that people have been conditioned by traditional diversity training to focus only on "soft" items like "Empathy," which is only part of the emotional intelligence equation. Actually, just about every sub-scale of the EQi had a significant positive correlation with at least one of the scales on the IDI. In other words, the more a person demonstrates emotional intelligence— controls impulses, manages stress, exhibits self-awareness, is flexible, shows optimism, accepts social responsibility—the more likely that person is to have an understanding and appreciation of relevant cultural differences. However, the revelation that Problem-Solving was the most significant driver caused me to rethink how the concept of diversity and inclusion has been approached in this country. I began to explore the brain deeply, how its design might be significantly contributing to Americans' challenge with connecting across racial lines. Diversity is not a "soft" concept. The significant problems we face demand whole-brain solutions.

Where do we Begin?

Taking the Problem-Solving approach that proved so effective in my study, I realize that everything starts with people understanding where they are in terms of their understanding and activity level around issues

CULTURAL KNOWLEDGE / ACTIVITY MATRIX

	Misinformed	Uninformed	Informed
Progressively Proactive	Re-Educate	Educate	Support
Progressively Reactive	Re-Educate	Educate	Support
Inactive	Re-Educate and Inspire	Educate and Inspire	Inspire and Support
Regressively Reactive	De-Radicalize and Re-Educate	Educate	Withdraw Support
Regressively Proactive	De-Radicalize, Re-Educate and Re-Direct	Educate and Re-Direct	Withdraw Support

of diversity. I have developed the Cultural Knowledge/Activity Matrix to model to help you with that process. The point of the model is that not everyone comes to the discussion from the same education base nor the same level of interest in the subject.

Informed people understand the concepts in this book, but vary in the degree to which they want to get involved to try to change things.

Uninformed people are either not interested, ambivalent, or in denial about issues of race relations, which is particularly true of some Whites who live and work in segregated communities where these issues don't affect their lives on a regular basis. Education is the goal.

Misinformed people are prone to believe information from unreliable sources. They have been fed bad data and bogus studies. They tune in to news programs, blogs, and radio talk shows that present biased information masquerading as facts. Education is the goal.

Progressively Proactive people are on the front lines. Many have sought out and accepted careers that enable them to advance this issue. People in this category are vocal, active, and spend a lot of time trying to convince others of the merits of their position.

Progressively Reactive people are those from whom you hear from only when there is a major news story or when something happens to them personally. They might even march in support of progressive policies and practices when high-profile incidents occur, but it is not something with which they engage on a regular basis.

Inactive people may feel bad and know that something wrong is happening, but they don't understand how to reverse the situation. Some inactive people feel that the issue is too big for them to try to tackle. Others are just too focused on the challenges of daily life to spend much time grappling with issues like race.

Regressively Reactive people are the ones you hear from only when there is a major news story or something happens to them personally. These people make good fodder for late might talk show hosts because they say things like, "I can't stand Obama Care, but I approve of the Affordable Healthcare Act." They are determined to "Take America Back"—either from someone who they believe "owns" the country, or back to a certain time when they believed things were better for them.

Regressively Proactive people are vocal and active, and spend a great deal of time trying to convince others of the merits of their position. People in this category are more likely to join militias and hate groups or commit hate crimes. You hear from them through their venom-filled rants in the comments section of news stories about racial incidents. They march in support of regressive policies and practices. A Regressively Proactive individual is more likely to draw a picture of President Obama depicted as a monkey and demand that he go back to Africa.

Progressively Proactive/Misinformed people, while their hearts are often in the right place, can often make situations worse. Some Liberal Whites who are motivated by guilt or anger fall into this box. Blacks who are motivated by anger or frustration might fall into this box. Without facts and a deep level of understanding of all the complexities involved in racial issues to back up those emotions, they risk becoming marginalized and having their concerns dismissed. Unfortunately, there are even diversity trainers who fit into this box. These individuals need education.

Progressively Proactive/Informed people are taking their passion for and knowledge about this issue to as many people as they can. They become teachers and professors at universities, employees at think tanks, civil rights leaders, nonprofit executives, and human resources professionals. While it would be great if most Americans could fit into this box, it is not realistic. Not everyone will have the same degree of passion about the subject, nor will they have the life circumstance that would enable them to devote time to this issue. These individuals need our support and appropriate platforms to get their message out.

Regressively Proactive and *Regressively Reactive* people in the *Misinformed* and *Uninformed* boxes are convinced that the stereotypes about Blacks are true, and they want everyone to know how they feel. Some of them believe Whites are genetically superior to Blacks. They are more likely to join hate groups and/or commit hate crimes. Ironically, they, too, are victims. They have been the targets of elite predators in America's ruling class throughout the history of the country to grow and maintain their wealth and influence.

The cause, then, of racial strife and quality-of-life disparities in America isn't White people as a group or rich people as a group. The problem is, and always has been, a small subset of very rich, very influential Whites, who I call the Predatory Elites, who have repeatedly demonstrated predatory instincts. I have often heard people in this category describe poor Black people as lazy, which is ironic. In some ways, it is really wealthy people who are lazy. They likely don't work 40-hour jobs and certainly not two jobs like some poor Blacks. They don't hold physically demanding jobs that are performed in the extreme heat and cold. They don't work difficult night jobs to get shift differential. They typically hire staff to handle all the housework and help with the kids. They have all the latest technology at their fingertips to make their lives easy and reduce the effort it takes to get things done. There are certainly people who pay their dues early in life to have these luxuries, but there are also many people who take these conveniences for granted because they have had them all of their lives. Very few of those people are Black.

Regressively Proactive/Informed people are the most despicable in America's history. Considering what we know about neuroscience, I will describe in this book how the Predatory Elite, who often know better, have created and continue to perpetuate America's tragic disparities through their neuro-manipulation of Blacks and working-class Whites. Individuals in this group are highly educated. As in the case of members of Congress, for instance, they have access to the most accurate information about issues of racial bias and discrimination. Experts testify before them and present all the findings from latest studies, but they often ignore that information when they go back to their districts. Instead of using the data that they have studied to correct misinformed persons at their rallies, they promote and spread the misinformation. Some of them flat out lie. They have decided the support of the voters is more important than the truth. Political leaders must be held to a much higher standard.

Brain Games

Once you understand which of the boxes in the Matrix best captures where you are regarding your knowledge and level of activity on issues of race, it is important to understand the mental tendencies that influence how people get in which box and how they stay there. To aid in such understanding, I will present information that is rarely used in the context of race. My goal is to change the conversation about race by helping people see these issues in a whole new light, which will open the door for new solutions to the problems we experience.

Almost everyone has seen the video where people are passing around a ball and the observer is to count how many passes there are among the individuals in the white shirts. This video was co-created by my fellow Cornellian, Daniel J. Simons, who now teaches in the Psychology Department at my Alma Mater, the University of Illinois. If you happen to be among the five or six people in the world who haven't seen the video, go look at it right now at http://www.theinvisiblegorilla.com/videos.html. In their book, *The Invisible Gorilla*, Dr. Simons and his colleague, Dr. Christopher Chabris, provide a great deal of insight into what's called "inattentional blindness," which is when someone fails to recognize an unexpected stimulus that is right in front of them (Chabris, & Simons, 2011). In the video, there is a gorilla that walks slowly across the screen. He stops in the middle of the passers and beats his chest. Observers are so busy counting the passes of the ball that they totally miss seeing the gorilla. I asked Dr. Simons if there were differences in whether people saw or didn't see the gorilla based on their background, education, training, or any other reason. He shared with me that, "There are remarkably few individual/group differences in noticing rates for this sort of task." The results, then, had nothing to do with intelligence or experience; it has more to do with how our minds work. The same holds true for the hundreds of optical illusions you can find by doing a quick Internet search. The illusions work on everyone from high school dropouts to PhDs because the human brain is predictable in how it processes certain information, regardless of intelligence level.

There are several ways that this invisible gorilla example might apply metaphorically to our issues with race. If you are not looking for something specific, or looking for something else, it could be easily missed. Similarly, confirmation bias occurs when one is consciously or subconsciously looking for individuals from a different background to be demonstrating stereotypical behavior, it would be easy to miss individuals from that background who may not be demonstrating that behavior. The example that I have used for years to demonstrate this behavior with audiences has to do with car shopping. Imagine going to the car dealership. Let us say you are an extrovert and want to buy something unique and eye-catching. The salesperson takes you around the showroom, and you come upon something that excites you. The car is a canary yellow (just stick with me on this one) coupe. You tell the salesperson that you have found your car. After a tough negotiation session, you buy the canary yellow car because it is uniquely you. As you drive out of the car lot, waiting for a break in the steady flow of traffic to proceed, to your dismay, three of the next ten cars happen to be canary yellow coupes! Your immediate reaction is to turn around and get your money back. After all, you wanted to buy something that was different, and it seems that everybody in town has a car like yours. Where were all of those damn canary yellow coupes before? Well, they were there all along, but you had no reason to notice them because there was no emotional connection between you and canary yellow coupes before you bought yours. You were reserving your valuable brain space for those things that matter to you most. Well, that is not quite accurate. The information was there somewhere, but there was no reason for it to be a part of your conscious thoughts. Your having not seen the yellow coupes before has nothing to do with your intellect or any other personal characteristic.

I believe scientists have unlocked many of the secrets that would help us move past our race problem in America, but they don't know it. Dr. Simons referred me to a different department when I told him that I was writing on the "neuroscience of racism." He indicated that he would be happy to help me, but he didn't know anything about that subject. I responded, "You know more than you think." Researchers haven't thought about applying concepts they have discovered to this new context. I believe inattentional blindness is one of those promising concepts. I have already pointed out that the country is still segregated, meaning there is little daily interaction across racial lines. As a keynote speaker, I have noticed that when I quote certain studies or mention particular sets of data, people in the audience are typically more familiar with the things that pertain specifically to their group. For instance, if I mention a study in which the researchers concluded that women are disproportionately underrepresented in a particular area, more women than men in the audience have heard of the study. The same pattern holds true for race. Because people are not dealing with these issues on a regular basis, it is not a focus of their attention, so they tend to miss some things that are right in front of them. It has little to do with being good or bad people, or even having reservations about other groups. People didn't miss the gorilla in the video based on their feelings about gorillas; they were counting passes, not looking for gorillas. I think many White Americans miss key facts about racial bias and discrimination simply because they are not actively looking for that information; they could be watching the news or reading the newspaper, but fail to "see" the stories that are right in front of them.

Stereotyping, in fact, is another concept that becomes very easy to understand if viewed through a scientific lens. The brain wants to work as efficiently as it possibly can to free up your attention for the stuff that affects your daily life. Peoples' perceptions are shaped by the connections they make among things they see each day. So Black people growing up in an all-Black community are probably not spending a whole lot of time thinking about Whites. When they do, they are prone to believe what they see on TV, the Internet, or whatever they read. They are also likely to believe that their experience with one White person gives them everything they need to know to understand all White people. Their brains have created "White" boxes. This is true for millions of things in day-to-day life. When I have to do a speech, for instance, if the lapel microphone looks like ones I used before, my brain wastes no energy figuring out how to use it. My brain has created a lapel microphone box. You can pick up any pen and write with it without having to put it in your mouth like an infant to figure out what it is because your brain has created a box for pens. So, while stereotyping can be dangerous and hurtful, our tendency to stereotype or generalize does not necessarily make us mean; it makes us human. Stereotyping is a shortcut the brain creates to free up capacity to think about other items.

The brain's shortcut doesn't just work when ascribing negative attributes to a group, even positive stereotypes can be damaging. Many Americans have bought into the idea that Asians are the "model minority," particularly regarding education. After all, China regularly leads all OECD nations on the Program for International Student Assessment (PISA) exam, which assesses math, science, and reading. However, there is a footnote. China, only shares the scores from Shanghai, where wealthy parents spend more per year on their children's education than what an average worker in China makes for the whole year (Stout, 2013). Shanghai's population comprises only about 1.7 percent of China's overall population. I remember having a conversation about this "model minority" idea with Anil, my Cornell classmate at Cornell. He commented on how he thought the idea was ridiculous. He suggested that people should go to India and meet some of his lazy, dumb relatives. "That is why they are still there and my mother and father came here," he joked. To Anil's point, about 27% of adults ages 25 to 64 in South Korea and 25% in Japan have a bachelor's degree or more. In contrast, nearly 70% of comparably aged recent immigrants from these two countries have at least a bachelor's degree (Pew Research Center, 2012). So, because the Asians we interact with in America are well educated, we assume that all Asians are well educated and place a higher value on education.

To avoid jumping to such assumptions requires one to be proactive to work against the brain's default efficiency mechanism. In other words, you must seek out experiences with people from all backgrounds to recognize a stereotype from an actual unique characteristic of that cultural group, and even then you have to understand that nothing can be applied to an entire group of people—there is always intra-group diversity. While this strategy seems straightforward, it is anything but easy. For example, I had an interesting discussion about race with a White female business owner several years ago while I was leading the City of Jacksonville's strategic visioning process. She had relocated her business to get away from Black people. She had dozens of people working for her business, but she indicated that she refused to hire any Black employees. She said that Black people were irresponsible and untrustworthy. She also added that they lacked any kind of work ethic. She went on to quote various negative statistics about Black people, particularly related to criminality.

After acknowledging some of her stats and correcting a few others, I asked her if she had ever fired any Whites for bad behavior. She indicated that she had. I also shared with her several negative stats about Whites, particularly related to criminality. She at first questioned my stats because she hadn't heard them. I shared sources with her, but she interrupted with, "It doesn't matter anyway. You are talking about 'White trash'. They have nothing to do with me." After chuckling a bit, I asked her if she thought it was fair for her to have "White trash," but I could not have "Black trash." She looked at me with a perplexed expression and admitted that she had never thought about it that way. This discussion perfectly illustrated how fragile the human mind can be. She had been programmed through her limited experience with Blacks to attribute bad behavior by them to their race, without attributing bad behavior by Whites to their race, but rather their class. Certainly, nobody in America, Black or White, should be looked at as trash, but the rules should be applied evenly.

MIRROR NEURONS AND AMYGDALA RESPONSE TO RACE

Scientists, such as Vilayanur Ramachandran, are exploring the existence of mirror neurons in the brain that are thought by some to be essential for people to connect with each other (2011). The mirror neurons of one person are thought to fire when he or she performs a particular task, or when he or she observes the same task being performed by someone else. In other words, watching someone drink a cup of water will stimulate activity in the observer's brain associated with drinking water. Mirror neurons make emotions contagious. Walk in a room with a smile on your face and watch as people respond with a smile. It goes even deeper than that. The theory works like this, consider two people having an exchange. Imagine a scientist has connected them both to a magnetic resonance imaging (MRI) machine and is reviewing the brain scans in another room. If one of the individuals is sharing information about a traumatic event he or she experienced, the scientist would actually be able to conclude that the individual speaking is talking about a traumatic event just by reading the scans. The individual speaking is reliving the experience to a degree as he or she speaks about it, and its effects can be seen in the area of the brain associated with stress and trauma. As if that wasn't fascinating enough, what is really surprising is that the scientist would also see activity associated with stress and trauma registering in the listener's brain. It's like the listener was there as well. Mirror neurons are thought by many researchers to be our built-in empathy mechanism. Think about the implications of our Facebook and Twitter culture. Without face-to-face human connection, what is happening to this system in the brain? No amount of emoticons can take the place of seeing the body language of an actual person.

Whites commonly assert, "I don't see race." New research on mirror neurons has revealed that even when people try to avoid consciously "seeing" race, the brain knows it is there. In a study where the subjects, Chinese and White, were stuck on the cheek by researchers with a stickpin or cotton swab, as long as a participant was observing someone of his or her own race, the mirror neurons worked as they should. However, the mirror neurons did not work the same across racial lines; the areas of the brain associated with pain did not register activity when a person from a different race from the observer was stuck with a stickpin. The researchers concluded, "Our findings have significant implications for understanding real-life social behaviors and provide a neuro-cognitive mechanism for stronger intentions to help racial in-group than out-group members" (Xu, Zuo, Wang, & Han, 2009). In other words, because I identify more closely with people who look like me, I am more likely to connect with and fell empathy for them.

In a similar study with Black and White participants, the researchers concluded, "The differential pain-specific empathic brain responses to in-group and out-group pain are linked to implicit racial bias." At unconscious levels, White people identified and empathized more effectively with Whites, and Black people identified and empathized more effectively with Blacks. The mirror neurons worked as long as the subjects and observers looked the same (Avenant, Sirigu, & Agliot, 2010). Maybe Founding Father Benjamin Franklin was on to something about race in America when he said, "Perhaps I am partial to the complexion of my country, for such kind of partiality is natural to mankind" (Observations Concerning the Increase of Mankind, Peopling of Countries, etc., n.d.).

While more research needs to be done before we can accept the existence and significance of mirror neurons, they may hold promising implications for how we understand race. Similar patterns have been observed associated with the amygdala, which is associated with fear and is so important to processing emotional information. In a review of neuroimaging studies of race-related prejudice that appeared in Frontiers in Human Neuroscience, the researchers found that prior research findings (Hart, Whalen, Shin, McInerney, Fischer, & Rauch, 2000; Phelps, O'Connor, Cunningham, Funayama, & Gatenby, 2000; Cunningham, Johnson, Raye, Gatenby, Gore, & Banaji, 2004; Wheeler and Fiske, 2005; Krill and Platek, 2009) support that the amygdala distinguishes between unfamiliar in-group and out-group faces at a subconscious level, with greater activity toward out-groups than in-groups. In other words Whites, for instance, had more activity in the amygdala when looking at pictures of Black people than when looking at pictures of White people. The researchers further noted that because of the negative culturally learned associations between Black males and potential threat, pictures of Black males, specifically, generated more activity in the amygdala (Chekroud, Everett, Bridge, & Hewstone, 2014).

I have trouble understanding why these kinds of studies don't find their way into the analysis of daily racial conflicts. I have heard no discussion of subjects such as mirror neurons and the way the amygdala deals with human differences in the ongoing dialogue about police shootings of unarmed Black boys and men. Based on this research, it is possible that a White officer's ability to identify with a Black suspect might be lower than that same officer's ability to identify with a White suspect, which could certainly influence the split-second decisions they have to make each day. The same could be true of Black officers. On top of the "normal" implications of mirror neurons, attitudes of superiority and inferiority further influence those split-second decisions, which explains why some Black officers may even be harsher to Black suspects. If one's assumption is that the cops in these situations are overtly racist, that assumption requires one set of solutions. If one's assumption is that race has nothing to do with these cases, that assumption requires a different set of solutions. None of these ideas have a chance of making any significant impact. New findings in neuroscience, such as how mirror neurons work across racial lines, could be helpful in finding the answers that are often buried somewhere between these two extremes.

Cultural Dynamics Model

Whites blame Blacks for not taking responsibility for self-destructive behavior. Blacks blame White privilege as the source of all the racial disparities in this country. I understand why the term "White privilege" strikes some Whites the wrong way. To "Joe the Worker," terms like "White privilege" are nonstarters, particularly if he is from a poor or working-class background. Emotions get involved. If I were a White working-class person, I would probably get upset about this term, too. The typical response from White people is, "Nobody ever gave me anything. I had to work hard for everything I have." To insinuate that successful Whites have not had to work hard to achieve their success is shortsighted; it only leads to guilt at best and resentment at worst. The problem is not that they didn't have to work, or that they got opportunities just because they are White—after all, they still had to compete against other Whites. The issue is that they weren't denied opportunities just for being Black. As pointed out in many examples in this book, Blacks can work just as hard but still achieve less impressive results because of biases. Too many Whites cannot see bias when it is there, and too many Blacks see it when it is not there. Because of this dynamic, the dominant culture unwittingly acts to maintain their dominance, while the non-dominant culture unwittingly acts to maintain their sub-ordinance. I have developed a model to illustrate this system and to help individuals understand the idea of "privilege" without having to use such a loaded term.

Culture is defined as "that pattern of knowledge, skills, behaviors, attitudes and beliefs, as well as material artifacts, produced by a human society and transmitted from one generation to another" (Pai & Adler, 2001, p. 21). In other words, culture is simply how people in a certain group think, what they do and how they connect with each other. As such, culture can refer to race, gender, sexual orientation, economic status, or religion. Culture can also be understood in broader terms like a team culture, organizational culture, or a community culture. Trying to describe a particular culture is a difficult and sometimes dangerous task.

Is what you are seeing a stereotype or rather a legitimate aspect of that culture? People conveniently latch on to positive characterizations about their culture, but they dismiss negative aspects as stereotypes. I will write more about what I call the "promise and perils" of culture later, but for purposes of understanding the model, think of culture as what people have in common and what connects them.

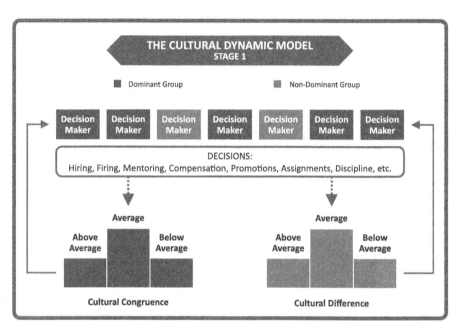

STAGE 1 STEP 1

At the top of the model are decision-makers, these are leaders who decide who gets a job and who is promoted, who goes to jail or goes free, who gets a passing grade and who doesn't, who qualifies for a loan and who doesn't, and so on. The darker squares represent the "dominant" group and the lighter squares represent the "non-dominant" group. The terms dominant and non-dominant, often referred to as majority and minority, simply refer to the number of people in that group who hold these positions. The model can be used to describe what happens with regard to race, gender, sexuality, height, weight, people from one school as opposed to another, people from different parts of the country, or any other cultural grouping. In America today, the dominant race would be White, the dominant gender would be male, the dominant religion would be Christian, the dominant sexual orientation would be straight, and so on. So, for instance, if people over 6 feet tall held more decision-making positions than people under 6 feet tall, people over 6 feet tall would be the dominant group. The left side of the model represents the dominant group; the right side of the model represents the non-dominant group.

Regardless of dominance or non-dominance, we seem to forget that most people are Average. Most people are average in terms of intellect, ability, work ethic, EI, or any other such characteristic. There is a small percentage Above Average people, a small percentage of Below Average people and the majority of us are in the middle somewhere, so the boxes on each side of the model are sized accordingly. As such, there is no reason to believe that, under equal circumstances, people in the non-dominant group should achieve any less in life than people in the dominant group.

Above Average

People who are above average have a higher degree of intellect, EI, drive, etc., than their peers.

Average

Most people do the best they can with what they have. They go to work, obey the law, pay their taxes, and take care of their families.

Below Average

People in this category lack the ability and/or desire to achieve great success.

STAGE 1 STEP 2

Now let's explore how hidden biases can affect outcomes for the dominant and non-dominant group. For this example, please put out of your mind any of the 'isms— racism, sexism, ageism, etc. Let's go back to the study cited earlier in this chapter regarding Black and White-sounding names. The bulk of the hiring managers in the study were probably White since Whites comprise the highest proportion of hiring managers in America, which makes them the dominant population. From my many years in human resources, I know that resumes are typically separated into three groups: "yes," "maybe," and "no" - in other words, "Above Average," "Average" and "Below Average." We know that something happened during this sorting process that resulted in some Above Average and Average resumes of applicants with Black-sounding names to be ranked lower than Above Average and Average resumes of White-sounding names. I believe too many people interpret the results to mean that these hiring officials consciously use race as a means to separate the groups. We know that this behavior is still present in America based on my discussion with the small business owner who said she would not hire Blacks, so it is likely that this behavior accounts for some of the difference in results, but I think individuals like her represent only a small percentage of people. I think studies such as this reveal something deeper, subtler, and more illusive.

It is important that we all understand that culture is something that is taken for granted like the air we breathe. When these hiring managers saw a name like Emily, it may have elicited a subconscious connection, particularly if they knew plenty of individuals named Emily. What if several of them had daughters or wives named Emily? On the other hand, the name Tamika would not have elicited the same positive emotional connection if they didn't know of any other Tamikas. Because the country is still segregated, it is unlikely that the White hiring managers would have known other Tamikas. Tamika might not have felt like a "good fit." Moreover, what if a hiring manager's only reference to the name Tamika is what they heard on the crime report on the nightly news? Even if there were crime reports with the name Emily, because of connections to other Emilys who were not criminals, those reports would not have cast a negative shadow over all individuals named Emily. All of this could have happened without the hiring officials being consciously aware of it. If someone were to go back and accuse them of being racist, they would likely get extremely offended. Having the name Emily in a country where the dominant racial group has many members with the name has some advantages; this is an example of what researchers and practitioners mean by "White privilege." To avoid the emotional response to the term, I instead refer to this dynamic as "cultural congruence."

Cultural congruence occurs when there is a connection between individuals based on a shared characteristic, experience, or belief. This phenomenon plays out every day in organizations across the country. Imagine that you are a hiring manager at a large, very successful company. You are a senior level male in the organization. You need to hire someone for an important position. For this position, you stressed to the human resources team to get you a diverse candidate pool because you believe in the value of workforce diversity. After reviewing the resumes, you narrow your choice down to two candidates —a male and a female. You are convinced that on paper either candidate has the background and experience to do the job, so you invite both for an interview.

Let's say the interview with the male candidate is first. The interview is going okay, but not stellar. Towards the end of the interview, the gentleman asks what you do for fun at the company. You share with him that tomorrow is an employee golf tournament at the local country club. He gets excited and explains to you that he loves the game and just played at the same club this past weekend. The two of you begin to talk about golf and your experiences at that club. All of a sudden an interview that was just so-so has just gotten much more interesting. The two of you shake hands and end the interview. Now it's the female candidate's turn. Unfortunately, just an in the first interview, there are no bells and whistles early in the discussion. Before she leaves, she happens to also ask what the company does for fun. You share with her about the golf tournament.

She says, "Oh, that sounds like a lot of fun. I hope you have a great time." The two of you shake hands and end the interview.

Who do you hire? If you are like most people, you hire the male candidate because he feels like a "better fit." If someone accused you of being sexist or discriminatory, you would likely blow a gasket. Nowhere in the scenario did I say you didn't like women or thought that a woman couldn't do the job as well as a man. As you made the decision, the issue of gender likely never popped into your mind. Yet, the connection was all about golf. Although there are women golfers, the disproportionate number of golfers is male, so men have an advantage if the subject of golf comes up in an interview— cultural congruence.

There are other examples that don't involve race, gender, age, or religion. I have already shared with you that I did my undergraduate work at the University of Illinois at Urbana-Champaign. When I see other "Illini," regardless of characteristics such as race or gender, I feel a kinship to them—cultural congruence. If I had to make a decision between two evenly matched candidates, a fellow Illini and a Missouri Tiger for instance, I'd have to work hard not to let that Illini connection drive my decision. It is unlikely that we would sit in an interview without discussing our experiences at Illinois. We would share stories about the dorms, Green Street, sports teams, and maybe even professors we had in common. I would have an opportunity to build a great rapport with the candidate based on our shared experience. Once I selected the Illinois graduate, I would justify my hiring decision as being based on the rapport that we developed in the interview. It would likely not occur to me that the rapport had its basis in the fact that we were both from Illinois. What if most of the hiring managers in America were University of Illinois graduates? It is a safe bet that Illinois students, compared to their peers from other schools, would have great jobs awaiting them post-graduation. I could provide dozens of examples of how well-meaning people can fall into this trap. If one accepts that this phenomenon exists, there has to be an associated acknowledgement that regardless of individual merit, people in non-dominant groups in America—Blacks, women, gays, Muslims, and so forth—are at a bit of a disadvantage, contrary to taking all of the jobs as some people believe. The likelihood of them making important connections and building rapport in interviews is lower than that of "mainstream" applicants.

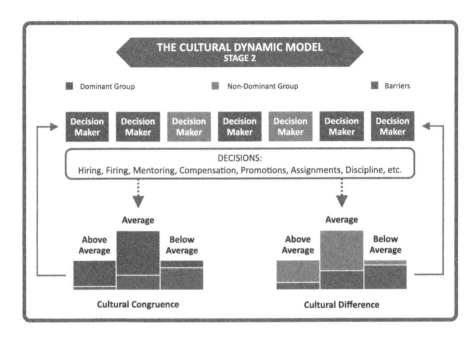

STAGE 2

In Stage 2 of the model, the shaded area at the bottom of the boxes represents the cumulative potential barriers to success for that group, or the likelihood that those group members will not succeed. Given all of this, lets explore what happens in each category.

Dominant/Above Average

These are smart, hardworking people. They routinely experience cultural congruence, so decisions are consistently made in their favor.

They are typically very successful. These are the future leaders in business and industry, education, medicine, etc. For whatever reason, there is a small percentage that will not achieve significant success.

Dominant/Average

These people do what they are supposed to do. They routinely experience cultural congruence, so decisions are sometimes made in their favor because of it. They frequently lose opportunities to **dominant/ above average** people, and sometimes to **non-dominant/above average** people, but they are generally successful.

Dominant/Below Average

These people lack the ability and/or drive to achieve great success. Even though they routinely experience cultural congruence, decisions are frequently not made in their favor. They routinely lose opportunities to **dominant/above average** people, frequently lose opportunities to **dominant/average** people and **non-dominant/above average** people, and sometimes lose opportunities to **non-dominant/average** people. People in this group consistently struggle to obtain the American Dream. Dr. Ruby Payne writes extensively about this group, providing a framework for understanding behaviors exhibited by this group. She points out that views among the people in this group are different from views of middle class and wealthy people regarding finances, cuisine, education, and a whole host of topics (Payne, 2005).

Non-Dominant/Above Average

These are smart, hardworking people. While many achieve great success, they are routinely passed over for opportunities in favor of **dominant/above average** people and frequently passed over in favor of **dominant/average** people because of cultural congruence. Think of the

"What Is in a Name" study here.

Non-Dominant/Average

These people play by the rules and do what they are supposed to do. They routinely lose opportunities, however, to **dominant/above average** people, and are frequently passed over in favor of **dominant/average** people and sometimes even **dominant/below average** people because of cultural congruence.

Non-Dominant/Below Average

This is the group that is struggling most in America. These people lack the ability and/or drive to achieve great success. Every group across the dominant and non-dominant spectrum experiences a higher level of success than this group in almost every quality of life indicator in the country. People in this group struggle with generational poverty. They are well aware of this fact, so many don't think it is worth it to try to change the story. While they may cite the primary reason for their failure as being in the non-dominant group, they would likely not be successful even if they were in the dominant group and Below Average.

On top of the individual challenges of people in this group, consider the circumstances in which many are born. Whites are more likely to be born in Above Average circumstances than Blacks, which provides a boost. If you have Average or Below Average abilities, but have Above Average resources, your chance of success is greater than if you have Average or Below Average abilities and born into Below Average circumstances. I am often reminded of this when I speak with people about their decision to put their kids in private schools. They put their kids in these schools precisely for the quality teaching and abundant resources that they feel will provide them with an advantage over their public school counterparts, yet when they outperform the public school kids, many parents attribute this difference in student outcomes to individual "merit" as opposed to better preparation.

Outliers

There are certainly people who fail despite having enormous resources, and others who achieve remarkable success despite growing up with nothing. People say things like, "Well, I was born in Below Average circumstances, but I made it, so that proves that anyone can." They also say things like, "I know a Black person who got a job over a more qualified White person." We tend to latch on to these outliers because they make us feel good, or enable us to deny that something is terribly wrong. I have even heard many Blacks say that we just have to accept that we have to work harder and be smarter than our White counterparts. While there will be exceptions, I feel strongly that there is no way we can reasonably expect people to do so en masse. To expect consistently extraordinary results from ordinary people is foolish.

The other argument I hear a lot regarding young people is that it's the parents' fault when things don't go right. I take parenting seriously—so much so that I believe people shouldn't have kids until after turning 30 years old when the frontal lobes of the brain are fully developed. However, we sometimes give too much credit to parents when things go right with their kids and too much blame when things go wrong. Neuroscientists suggest that a significant part of a parent's work is already done by the day they leave the hospital with their new bundle of joy. Technically, genetics is the dominant determinate of who we become, accounting for over 50% of individual physical and behavioral characteristics (Howard, 2006). I will provide more insights on practical aspects of nurture vs. nature later, but sticking with the idea of nature, some of the best examples can be found in studies of identical twins. Twins separated at birth and raised in completely different environments consistently show strong similarities in lifestyle, occupations, and religious feelings. In one example, previously separated twins were interviewed when they were twenty-seven years old. Though they had no contact with each other since birth, both were obsessive-compulsive "neat freaks." When asked what drove this behavior, they both attributed it to the influence of their adoptive parents. One of the twins said it was because his adoptive parents were slobs, and he did not want to be a slob like them. The other twin said it was because his adoptive parents were neat freaks, so he made sure he was always neat. Therefore, no matter what household these twins would have grown up in, they were likely destined by the genetic contributions of their birth parents to be neat freaks (Neubauer & Neubauer, 1990).

To further illustrate that parents might not have as much impact as one may think, consider that nurture is technically composed of two influences: shared and non-shared experiences (Wright, 1998). Shared experiences include the activities that parents do with all the kids together. Playing the piano for the kids each night is a shared experience, for instance. According to scientists, the shared experiences matter less in determining who we become than one might think (Howard, 2006). Non-shared experiences, such as a boy's father taking him fishing on the weekends while his sister hangs out with mom, are significant. It is through these unique, non-shared experiences that we begin to understand who we are and how we individually relate to the world. Surprisingly, the primary source of non-shared experiences is not inside the home at all, but rather it's the child's salient peer group (Howard, 2006). More on this later, but the gist is that Granny was right about being selective about who you decide to hang out with.

SUMMARY

If people are really smart, born into wealth, or work really hard—in other words are Above Average—they will likely succeed in America regardless of whether they belong to the dominant or non-dominant group. Cultural congruence is negligible in determining the success of Above Average people. We also know that if people are born poor and/or have a poor work ethic or Below Average smarts, they will probably not be successful regardless of whether they belong to the dominant or non-dominant group. Cultural congruence is negligible in determining the success of Below Average people too. The challenge is most obvious with dominant and non-dominant Average people, the category in which most Americans fall. Simply put, if one group has more hurdles than another, fewer people from that group will succeed. Success often results in one becoming a decision-maker, so the cycle perpetuates itself.

Keep in mind that this entire discussion has been focused primarily on what happens on an unconscious or "hidden" level. We cannot continue to label people as evil and sneaky on one side or immoral and lazy on the other side. We cannot continue to have too many Whites deny that cultural congruency is part of what is happening and too many Blacks feeling that this it is the only influence in action. The consequences of this narrow-minded thinking have been devastating.

CHAPTER 5

The Predictable Result: Persistent Traumatic Stress

The more refined and subtle our minds,
the more vulnerable they are.
—Dr. Paul Tournier

2016 U.S. Presidential hopeful Dr. Ben Carson is an extraordinary man. He overcame poverty and prejudice to become one of the world's top neurosurgeons. I met Dr. Carson while attending a conference where he was the keynote speaker. I shared with him that I was working on the first edition of this book at the time, and he graciously agreed to provide me with some feedback. I sent him the manuscript a few days later, and to his word, he wrote me back with some advice. I was so impressed that a man as busy as he would find the time to do this for me. Now that he is running for president, Carson is on the speaking circuit. I recently heard one of those radio interviews and I have read several excerpts from his speeches. In the interview, Carson spoke about the destruction of the Black family, disrespect for the law, and poor educational attainment. I agree that the behavior he described is highly problematic. It is what he didn't say that bothers me, particularly given the audience he was addressing—a predominately White, Misinformed and Uninformed, Regressively Active, and Regressively Reactive group on talk radio.

I cannot speak to Carson's motivations since I only met him briefly, but I disagree with his actions. Speaking to predominately White audiences admonishing the "bad behavior" of Black people gives Whites who are prone to discriminate a free pass, and lets Whites who feel compelled to help off the hook. Carson made two significant errors in his discussion: (1) he failed to acknowledge that Black people do not hold a patent on poverty and destructive behavior and (2) he failed to point out where such behavior gets its genesis. In a recent letter to Carson, I wrote:

The very term "African American community" is problematic. Just as the White population or any other group is diverse, one can think of Black people in at least three buckets: (1) people who, despite the legacy of racism, have achieved significant professional and financial success; (2) lawful, responsible people who work hard to make ends meet; and (3) people who fit the many negative stereotypes with which the "African American Community" is saddled.

These categories are equivalent to Above Average, Average, and Below Average in my Cultural Dynamics Model. Critics like Carson imply that the majority of Blacks are Below Average people. I went to a presentation several years ago to listen to *Fox News* contributor Juan Williams after he published his book, *Enough* (2006). Consistent with Dr. Carson's sentiments, the theme of Williams' discussion was, "What would Dr. King do?" His point was that Dr. King would be appalled at the destructive behavior among Blacks today. Williams specifically gave the example of music videos. He said that King would be heartbroken to tune in to Black Entertainment Television (BET) to see scantily dressed Black women dancing provocatively to offensive hip-hop songs. What Williams failed to point out is that all King would have had to do is flip through the channels to see naked White women, not only dancing provocatively, but actually *having* sex. What would Dr. King have said about shows such as *Jerry Springer* and *Judge Judy* where the participants are predominantly White? Why would Dr. King hold Blacks to a higher standard than anyone else? Again, holding Average people to Above Average standards is a recipe for disaster. The real issue here is that there are few images of Blacks on TV, so it is easy to generalize their behavior to all Black people. I call this the "Law of the Subgroup." There are hundreds of channels depicting Whites across a range of activities, so one image or activity, regardless of how distasteful, does not reflect on the "White Community" the same way one image or activity seems to reflect on the "Black Community."

I often hear "crabs in a barrel" as a description to illustrate how Blacks hold each other back. People don't describe Whites that way, yet every day in courtrooms all across America, Whites are trying to sue the pants off other Whites—sometimes their own family members. We ignore that Bernie Madoff, for example, made his fortune by exploiting other Jewish Americans. White methamphetamine and heroine dealers sell drugs to other Whites every day. Consider the phrase "Black on Black Crime," which has been generally accepted as an indication of the level of self-hate in the Black community. It is true that 92% of the time when Blacks are murdered, the perpetrator is Black, but what most people don't know is that 86% of the time when Whites are murdered, the perpetrator is White (FBI, n.d.). Nobody talks about "White on White Crime." As a practical matter, if someone is going to commit a violent crime against you, it will be someone of your own race. The problem, then, is not so much "Black on Black Crime," but rather the high level of crime in poor inner-city communities that are predominantly Black as a result of redlining and other systemic and structural issues. Of course there is crime in rural, predominantly White communities as well. Poverty is a major factor contributing to undesirable behaviors in these communities just as it is in inner-cities. One of the reasons that people associate these behaviors only with Blacks is that the media doesn't highlight remote places where struggling Whites live. Moreover, people don't go to these communities unless they live there, so this behavior is often "hidden." Look at the covers of the annual reports of your local poverty-fighting nonprofits, or watch the television commercials where people are seeking donations or volunteers. Invariably, there will be many images of Black kids or Black families, giving people the impression that poverty has a Black face in America. However, in 2013, there were 19,027,400 Whites in poverty compared to 10,312,400 Blacks in poverty (Henry J. Kaiser Family Foundation, n.d.). Certainly given the size of the population, Blacks are struggling disproportionately as it relates to poverty and its associated destructive behaviors, but given that poor Whites outnumber poor Blacks by nearly a 2 to 1 margin, there should be some White faces on the advertisement of some of these poverty programs. Otherwise, the message communicated to donors is that poverty is a "Black thing"—a natural consequence of being inferior. While poverty is not just a Black problem, the country has got to get a better grip on understanding why Blacks are disproportionately poor.

Stress: A Formidable Opponent

Admittedly, I did not have a healthy respect for stress as a young manager in Corporate America. When people on my team would complain about stress I would quickly dismiss their complaints. I viewed stress as an excuse for people not perform at high levels, so my patience for people struggling with it was low. Fortunately, I have learned a great deal about stress over my professional career. I have seen how debilitating it can be for people. I have learned that human beings respond to stress in some very predictable ways, which I describe in a continuum that I developed.

MENTAL HEALTH AND STRESS CONTINUUM			
	BEHAVIORAL SIGNS	PHYSICAL SIGNS	EMOTIONAL SIGNS
Stage 1 WELL	Prepared Respectful Eager to Learn Sociable Adaptable	Healthy Active	Confident Optimistic
Stage 2 STRESSED	Over or Under-Eating Drug or Alcohol Use Smoking Relationship Conflicts Trouble Focusing	Headaches Back Pain Heart Issues High Blood Pressure Decreased Immunity Upset Stomach Weight Gain or Loss Problems Sleeping	Underprepared Irritable Anxious Passive Withdrawn Untrusting Inconsistent Unsure
Stage 3 DISTRESSED	Stage 2 Signs Social Withdrawal Angry or Sad Outbursts Forgetfulness Worrying Irritability Lack of Focus	Stage 2 Signs Other Chronic Health Issues	Stage 2 Signs Disrespectful Detached Inflexible Negative Frightened Pessimistic Insecure Hopeless
Stage 4 MENTALLY ILL	Stage 3 Signs Others Specific to Diagnosis	Stage 3 Signs Others Specific to Diagnosis	Stage 3 Signs Others Specific to Diagnosis

At one end of the spectrum is optimal mental health, which only 17% of the people in the country enjoy according to the United Sates Department of Health and Human Services (1999). At the other end of the spectrum are mental challenges so severe that they make daily life very difficult. Over the course of the average person's life, numerous serious mental health issues could adversely affect him or her. There are disorders like attention-deficit/hyperactivity disorder (ADHD), autism spectrum disorders, dyslexia, epilepsy, retardation, schizophrenia, stuttering, and brain tumors. There are disorders brought on by injury or catastrophic events like abused child syndrome, concussions, headaches, post-traumatic stress disorder (PTSD), spinal cord injury, and strokes. There are degenerative diseases like Alzheimer's, Creutzfeldt-Jakob, Huntington's, amyotrophic lateral sclerosis (ALS), Lyme disease, multiple sclerosis, and Parkinson's. As if that is not enough, there are also mood disorders and addictions such as anxiety, depression, bipolar disorder, seasonal affective disorder, and eating disorders. With all of these potential ailments, it is a miracle that any of us are "normal." Well, we are all normal if normal includes having some problems. Remember that 87% of us are at less than optimum mental health. Moreover, nearly 25% of Americans have a mental disorder in any given year. About half of us will have a disorder at some point in our lives, but less than 40% of the affected people will seek help (National Alliance on Mental Illness, 2003; Reinberg, 2011). As with any illness, stress is a leading contributor. Over 60% of human illness and disease claims stress as its basic cause (The American Institute of Stress, 2014).

The behavioral, physical, and emotional toll stress takes on us is enormous. Nearly 80% of the population regularly experiences symptoms of stress (American Psychological Association (APA), 2012). On top of this routine stress for which every American is at risk, add the stress associated with being a Black person in America. Think about all that you have read in this book—slavery, lynching, Jim Crow, red-lining, as well as discrimination in employment, education, healthcare, and law enforcement—virtually every facet of life. The result is fairly clear. Stress has nearly KO'd Black America.

PREDICTABLE RESPONSES TO STRESS

I am not interested in making excuses for people. I am, however, interested in discovering legitimate, data-driven, mind/brain-related reasons why people behave the way they do. Just as we can predict that people will fall for those optical illusions I wrote about earlier in the book, there are some important inferences we can make about human behavior. The public has fallen in love with television crime shows, such as *Criminal Minds*. Although sometimes over-sensationalized for entertainment purposes, these shows give viewers a glimpse into complex patterns of human behavior.

The Federal Bureau of Investigation (FBI) began practicing behavioral profiling in the 1950s. Though some question its efficacy and worry that it may be a mask for racial profiling, law enforcement officials claim to use behavioral profiling to solve cases all over the world by pinpointing various aspects of an unidentified perpetrator's life, such as relationship to the victim, interests, personality type, type of work, and other characteristics. The level of detail that criminal profilers can supply seems mind-boggling until you think about how predictable people are. Consider Stockholm syndrome, domestic abuse, and mob mentality, just to name a few areas where this strange but predictable phenomenon has been observed.

Stockholm syndrome is what happens when kidnapped victims ultimately begin to identify with their captors. The name comes from a 1973 incident in Stockholm, Sweden, where hostages at a bank began to thwart rescue attempts and refused to testify against their captors. Since then, there have been several well-documented cases of this phenomenon, including that of newspaper heir Patty Hearst who, after being kidnapped in 1974 by the Symbionese Liberation Army, joined them in committing several robberies (Namnyak, Tufton, Szekely, Toal, Worboys, & Sampson, 2008). There was also the case of Natascha Kampusch, who after being held from age ten until age 18, grieved after her captor committed suicide in 2006 (Ex-kidnap girl "sorry for captor," 2007). Despite speaking to the police on two separate occasions for unrelated matters, Shawn Hornbeck, who was abducted in 2002 and held for four years by Michael J. Devlin, did not inform police of his situation (Reynolds, 2007). Colleen Stan, who was abducted in 1977 at the age of 20, was repeatedly abused mentally and sexually, and she was forced to sleep in small box under her captor's bed for seven years. Incredibly, Stan stayed with her captors even though she had many opportunities to leave (McGuire, & Norton, 1989). While most of us believe we would respond differently, a surprising number of us—White, Black, rich, or poor—would respond in the very same manner as the individuals above.

Regardless of race or economic status, researchers have long reported that one-third of children who grow up in abusive households will grow up to abuse and neglect their own children (Safe Horizon, n.d.). While this fact seems paradoxical, it is easy to understand why this happens when you consider the fragility of the human brain. Kids who grow up in this situation consciously or subconsciously perceive abuse as a normal aspect of family life, so they naturally mimic what they see without even thinking about it. Many will indicate that they realize that abuse is wrong, but they find it difficult to modify their behavior given the psychological toll the violence has taken on them. It is easy to throw the book at someone who has abused a child, and abusers should be punished, but wouldn't it make more sense to give them the help they need before they commit the crime?

Mob mentality is another example of predictable behavior that knows no race or economic status. Mob mentality occurs when individuals do things with a group that they would normally never consider doing on their own. Interestingly, this behavior occurs in good times and bad. We can all remember the devastating LA riots of 1992 and the recent issues in Baltimore. While I do not condone the behavior, I can understand why these riots happened. People were angry and looked for a way, albeit an inappropriate one, to vent that anger. American history is littered with examples of mob mentality related to issues of race. From cross-burnings to riots, people have used the anonymity of the crowd to behave in despicable ways.

It is much more difficult, though, to come to grips with mob mentality during the good times. Euphoric fans turn over cars, loot, and trash their cities after their sports teams win championships. Sometimes the euphoria turns into tragedy. In 2004, a young college student died, and fifteen other people were hurt in Boston when thousands of baseball fans rioted in celebration of the Red Sox dramatic come-from-behind win over the Yankees for the American League pennant. Admittedly, I felt like rioting myself after they went on to dominate my beloved St. Louis Cardinals in the World Series.

As I indicated, mob mentality affects all races, but it is puzzling how people can't understand why Black people might riot when they believe the legal system has let them down. People are quick to say, "How can they think it makes sense to destroy their own communities?" Yet, riots featuring jubilant White fans after championships draw little news coverage or widespread public ire. Even the way people describe behaviors such as looting has been problematic in the press. For example, in the aftermath of Hurricane Katrina, a young Black male wading through chest-high water carrying a case of soda and pulling a bag was described as a looter, while two Whites carrying bags of food through the same flood waters were described as having found food from a grocery store (Ralli, 2005).

COMPLEX TRAUMA

The problems Black Americans are experiencing are fairly easy to understand based on what we know about the brain and human psychology. Individuals respond in some predictable ways to the stress of growing up in a place like East St. Louis, which has been described as "a scar of sorts, an ugly metaphor of filth and overspill and chemical effusions, a place for Blacks to live and die within" (Kozol, 1991, p. 39). As described in the "Perpetual Disparity Cycle" I introduced in Chapter 3, the cumulative effect of the Black experience in America has taken its psychological toll, especially on kids. Given all of this, it is not astonishing that many Black people in America are struggling.

Complex trauma occurs when children have been exposed to multiple or prolonged traumatic events. This type of trauma affects a child's physiological responses, as well as the social and emotional skills that are critical for personal and professional success. This type of trauma affects a child's ability to think, learn, and concentrate. Complex trauma is often overlooked in children because there is currently no diagnosis that adequately captures the range of child trauma effects (Griffin, & Studzinski, 2010). Many children who have experienced complex trauma don't meet the criteria for a diagnosis of PTSD. If this issue is not effectively addressed in childhood, it manifests itself into a whole host of adult problems including low job performance, substance abuse, chronic physical conditions, depression and anxiety, self-harming behaviors, and other psychiatric disorders (National Child Trauma Stress Network, n.d.). In fact, adults who experience six or more adverse childhood experiences were likely to die 20 years sooner than those with no adverse childhood experiences (Brown, Anda, Tiemeier, Felitti, Edwards, Croft, & Giles, 2009). Understanding the adult complications from childhood exposure to violence and abuse is why I cringe when I hear people say that its the parents' responsibility in these challenged communities to get their act together and take care of their families. Is it a reasonable expectation for a parent who has experienced complex stress to understand what they need to do to be a great parent? Many of these parents are hardly equipped to attend to even the most basic physical and emotional needs of their children. Individuals who do not outwardly exhibit the symptoms resulting from complex trauma may indirectly pass on these feelings of anger, resentment, insecurity, and despair. Therefore, this condition is can be passed down for generations.

When parents try to do what they believe is right in America's "traumatized" communities, the odds are stacked against them. I wrote earlier about leading Jacksonville's comprehensive strategic visioning process in 2005. An important component of the process was conducting several meetings with citizens to educate them regarding some of the discouraging trends we were seeing in the city, such as mediocre K-12 results, and to get their thoughts on how to address these issues. At one of the meetings, one of the participants said, "Look, what this boils down to is parental responsibility, plain and simple!" Participants, including educators, businesspeople, stay-at-home parents, and community volunteers began to nod their heads in agreement. Several of them echoed the comments of how devastating poor parenting and the lack of parental involvement had been on the paltry educational achievement of the city's kids. In the midst of all of this discussion, a middle-aged Black woman slowly raised her hand.

She was clearly nervous about speaking. Her voice trembled as she stared down at the table unable to make eye contact with the other participants. She said, "I have been a member of the PTA for years." She continued, "The teachers at my kids' school know me because I am there all the time. I understand what y'all are sayin' about the parents, but even though I really wanted them to finish school, my two sons dropped out of school in the ninth grade. I did the best I could, but it didn't help." Clearly, the kids in the neighborhood, their salient peer groups, had more of an influence on her kids than did she. The air in the room grew heavy. The group had allowed themselves to be worked into a frenzy based on their narrow perception of what the problem was. The parents in the room, who were from vastly different backgrounds, wanted to believe that they had a great deal of influence on their own kids' success, so parenting must be the key. What some of the participants later admitted was that they really hadn't had success with all of their kids either.

PERSISTENT TRAUMATIC STRESS ON AMERICA'S URBAN BATTLEFIELDS

Consider what happens to soldiers who go to war. These young adults undergo rigorous training to be ready for the test of physical and mental endurance they are about to experience, as well as the horrible images they are likely to see. Even with all the great training they receive, many are unprepared for the reality of combat. They see kids with bombs strapped to them. They see little old women toting machine guns. They see dead bodies in mass graves. They watch their fellow soldiers tortured and killed. They know at any time it could be their number called. Death, destruction, and despair become a way of life. Killing and dodging death becomes routine. Returning soldiers sometimes describe how the line between good and bad becomes blurred. For some, understanding right and wrong grows increasingly difficult to navigate. To survive, soldiers sometimes become people they don't even recognize.

Many who survive this horrible ordeal end up with life-altering physical injuries, such as missing limbs. The most common injury is that which occurs in their heads. Nearly 20% of veterans who have served in Iraq or Afghanistan since October 2001 have been diagnosed with PTSD (Darling, 2008). If 20% report symptoms of PTSD, just imagine how many veterans experience these symptoms but don't tell anyone. Some sufferers have minor symptoms like difficulty sleeping. Others have trouble concentrating or remembering. Some experience more troubling symptoms like violence against themselves or others. Substance abuse is high among those with PTSD. Many people with PTSD report having no hope for their future. A large body of research indicates that there is a correlation between PTSD and suicide (Hudenko, 2007).

PTSD is not just about fighting in foreign wars. It can affect almost anyone. About 25% of persons who are exposed to catastrophic events in the U.S. will develop PTSD at some point in their lives (Rosenberg, Mueser, Friedman, Gorman, Drake, Vidaver, Torrey, & Jankowski, 2001). In any given year, about 3.6 percent of Americans are suffering from this condition (PTSD Foundation of America, n.d.). Ultimately, the symptoms lead to behaviors that not only threaten one's quality of life, but also threaten people's lives altogether. Over time, PTSD strips individuals of their physical, spiritual, and mental health, and sometimes their freedom. According to Human Rights Watch, one in six prisoners in the U.S. is mentally ill (2003). The rate of mental illness in prisons is over three times the rate of mental illness in the general population. These numbers, while alarming, only account for mental conditions like bipolar disorder, depression, and schizophrenia. Imagine how many prisoners are suffering from the effects of PTSD, which assaults the brain's hippocampus, the part of the brain necessary for learning, forming new memories, and regulating the stress response (Southwick, & Charney, 2012). As a result of PTSD, the stress hormone cortisol is believed to initiate "a vicious cycle by creating a brain that becomes predisposed to be in a constant state of fight-or-flight" (Bergland, 2014). Imagine the number of people in America's criminal justice system who are suffering from this condition, which is likely exacerbated in a prison environment often ruled by violence, isolation, and fear. Violence, isolation, and fear are not characteristics that can be limited to war zones or prisons.

When I was a child, I saw the lifeless body of someone who had been stabbed. I later saw someone get shot in my house as my mother and I ran out. I knew dozens of people who have been murdered, several of them from my high school class. How is witnessing violence, death, and destruction any different whether it happens in Iraq or East St. Louis? Complex trauma and PTSD have to be prevalent in these communities. I don't mean to minimize at all what soldiers face in traditional war zones because what they endure is incredible. I am just indicating that nobody should be surprised when they see behaviors in America's challenged communities that mirror the symptoms of PTSD. These domestic "war zones" have rendered many "walking wounded."

Chronic stress literally changes people. Researchers in the field of epigenetics, which focuses on heritable changes in gene expression that do not involve changes in the DNA, suggest that stress can trigger biomedical reactions that then turn genes on or off (Southwick, & Charney, 2012). It is important to note that such stress affects not only the people living in these communities, but also the police who patrol them. PTSD is a major factor in the high rate of police suicides, which range from 125 to 150 each year. That is a rate of 17 per 100,000 compared to 11 per 100,000 for the general public (Badge of Life, n.d.). Just as I have heard no discussion of mirror neurons, I have heard little about PTSD as a possibility for some of the aggressive behavior of police in the shooting incidents that continue to garner national coverage. Is it not conceivable that instead of killing themselves, people who are struggling to cope could choose to lash out at others?

In *The World is Flat*, Thomas Friedman (2005) points out that individuals are more trusting, inclusive, and open to change when they feel that their and their children's futures are promising. Well, few parents in difficult communities have hope for themselves, let alone their kids. The kids don't believe that they have a bright future either, so they do not try. Doesn't this help explain why some young people would so casually throw their lives away committing senseless crimes that they know will get them killed or jailed? Just as in a traditional combat zone, violence becomes so routine that the line between good and bad is blurred. For them too, right and wrong grows increasingly difficult to navigate. Again, my goal is not to make excuses for people. I want to point out what is really happening as opposed to what we want to believe is happening. The research supports what I am seeing. In one study, PTSD was diagnosed among 29% of urban youths who witnessed, experienced, or lived with the threat of neighborhood violence (Berton, & Stabb, 1996).

The reason for the negative behaviors that Dr. Carson and others describe as prevalent in the Black Community becomes much more clear after taking into account what we now know about complex trauma and PTSD. Individuals with PTSD have high levels of cortisol, which pumps them up on adrenaline (Howard, 2006). Such individuals have "atypical brainwave activity, reduction in the size of the hippocampus, over-action of the amygdala, excessive arousal of the sympathetic nervous system and production of higher-than-average levels of bodily opiates" (Howard, 2006, p. 391). Some people under excess trauma are like bombs waiting to explode. The only certain way to elude PTSD is to avoid witnessing or becoming a target for violence, trauma, and/or severe distress. Unfortunately, kids living in traumatized families and communities have little or no control over the traumatic events that they will witness. PTSD is just one of the challenges that affect people in the inner cities of America.

"Anticipatory stress" describes the feeling that military spouses feel when their partners leave home to go fight. It is the feeling that doom is imminent. Imagine waiting for the phone to ring with bad news on the other side or looking through the window expecting the arrival of military officials to tell you that your loved one has been killed in combat. As they watch war coverage on television, hear stories on the radio, or read accounts of the war, their brains release harmful chemicals that assault their bodies and make daily life challenging. Similar to the spouses of combat soldiers, parents in America's traumatized communities feel this kind of anxiety every day their children walk outside to play or go to school. The young people feel it, too. Hip-hop superstars The Notorious B.I.G. (Christopher Wallace) and 2Pac (Tupac Shakur) each predicted that they would die violent deaths—and they did. Imagine what their lives must have been like. Despite having achieved remarkable professional and financial success, the thought of a violent death consistently loomed over them. Surely, struggling young people in these communities have the same ominous feeling. As such, individuals in these circumstances do not give anyone the benefit of the doubt. Trust is a scarce resource. Drama seems to follow them everywhere, and they desperately try to pull others into that negative mindset. They feel the world, including family and friends, has forsaken them, so they vow not to be taken advantage of by anyone. Conversely, they may be so weak and broken that they let everyone take advantage of them. This is not a new concept.

According to the United Nation's Istanbul Protocol Manual on the effective investigation and documentation of torture and other cruel, inhuman or degrading treatment or punishment, someone who has experienced extreme trauma often "has a sense of foreshortened future without expectation of a career, marriage, children, or normal lifespan" (Istanbul Protocol, 1999, p. 47). The phrase "sense of foreshortened future" is also mentioned as a symptom of post-traumatic stress disorder (PTSD) in the fourth edition of the Diagnostic and Statistical Manual of Mental Disorders (DSM-IV-TR, p. 468). While that language does not appear in the DSM-5, psychiatrists such as Dr. Steven Southwick, Professor of Psychiatry, PTSD and Resilience at Yale University School of Medicine and Yale Child Study Center, continue to address this issue with their patients. Dr. Southwick shared with me that this "sense of a foreshortened future" is a common characteristic of many of his patients who have experienced trauma.

PTSD and anticipatory stress only tell part of the story. Consider the collective depression that gripped people all over America after September 11, 2001. Many of us still have not recovered. Experts call this phenomenon "vicarious traumatization." As I have described, mirror neurons cause our bodies to undergo chemical changes when we listen to accounts of traumatic events from people with whom we identify (Gore, 2008). Think about the implications for Black people who watch documentaries about Civil Rights or programs like *Roots* or hear stories from their parents and grandparents about how Black people were severely mistreated in America's past. Because of "vicarious traumatization," some researchers argue that the impact of slavery is more direct than most people understand. Dr. Joy DeGruy-Leary believes that Blacks are suffering from "post traumatic slave syndrome" (PTSS), which she defines as, "A condition that exists as a consequence of multigenerational oppression of Africans and their descendants resulting from centuries of chattel slavery" (n.d.). The tragic stories that routinely unfold on the nightly news highlighting Black people as being both victims and perpetrators of violent crimes may trigger vicarious traumatization in young people who watch these programs. They see young people who look like them get carted away in handcuffs. The adults see mothers and fathers who look like them in despair and feel their pain – literally!

Americans didn't always understand the seriousness of PTSD. During the Civil War, it was described as "homesickness," only something the weakest of soldiers would exhibit (Bentley, 2005). Now, we know that it would be foolish to tell soldiers suffering from PTSD to just shake off the effects of what they have seen and take personal responsibility for their actions. It is universally accepted that they need and deserve professional help. Moreover, we wouldn't dare tell a woman who has been sexually assaulted to just get over it, or a child that has been severely abused to just forget about what happened. Why, then, do we expect people in

America's war zones to "shake off" the effects of what they have seen and experienced. I am not suggesting that anyone should get a free pass for breaking the law. If a soldier comes home with PTSD and commits a crime, we do not let him or her go free. I am suggesting that the collective "we" should take proactive steps to address the underlying psychological problems that produce destructive behaviors before the inevitable bad decisions are made.

There are potentially hundreds of thousands of individuals living in poor, urban communities across America suffering from a combination of complex stress, anticipatory stress, vicarious traumatization, and PTSD. Each of these conditions collude to produce what I call persistent traumatic stress (persistent-TS), which is tantamount to a noxious gas that infiltrates the city limits of East St. Louis and inner cities of places like St. Louis, Baltimore, Chicago, South Central Los Angeles, Detroit, Newark, and Jacksonville, Florida. The literal poisons in the soils coupled with the literal and figurative poison in the air produces a lethal combination that assaults the physical, social, and emotional health of the citizens in these communities. Some Above Average people have the inner strength to fight off the contaminant's effects, but most people are destined to fall victim to its fumes. These toxins hijack the mind, body and soul. Under these circumstances, it is easy to see why a smile, the product of hope and joy, is so difficult to come by in these communities.

IT STARTS IN THE WOMB

One of the most visible areas of racial disparities in America is infant mortality. In 2005, the rate of infant deaths per 100,000 people in the population was 13.8 for Blacks and 5.7 for Whites (MacDorman, & Matthews, 2013). After decades of studying this issue, there has been no clear explanation of why Black babies have significantly worse birth outcomes than do White babies. Most studies have focused on socioeconomic status, maternal risky behaviors, perinatal care, psychosocial stress, or perinatal infections during pregnancy (Singh & Yu, 1995). However, none of these reasons account for the difference in infant mortality. Black women of high socioeconomic status still have higher infant mortality rates than do White women with low socioeconomic status (Singh & Yu, 1995). Studies have shown, however, that not only are Black women less likely to smoke during pregnancy, Black women who did not smoke during pregnancy still had higher infant mortality than White women who did (Matthews, MacDorman, & Menacker, 2002). Cigarette smoke contains over 4,000 chemical components that can negatively affect an infant's development, including significantly lower IQs due to the reduced oxygen flow to the brain. Infants of cigarette smokers also have "lower birth weights, smaller brains, and poorer spatial and visual-motor skills" (Howard, p. 181). Moreover, fetal alcohol syndrome has a major affect in later life for most people. According to Howard, "90% of those born with this syndrome later have mental health problems, 60% have trouble with the law, 50% are involuntarily confined, and 50% are accused of inappropriate sexual behavior" (p. 77). There is also no evidence that there is greater alcohol or drug use among pregnant Black women (Singh & Yu, 1995). Black women who initiated prenatal care in the first trimester still had higher rates of infant mortality than did White women who had late or no prenatal care at all (Matthews et al.,2002). While it is generally known that stress during pregnancy can cause issues such as increased risk of low birth weight and preterm delivery, in one study, Black women who did not report experiencing more stress during pregnancy than White women still had higher infant mortality rates (Savitz & Pastore, 1999). Black women have higher rates of many lower urogenital tract infections and higher rates of amniotic infections, but the disparities in infant mortality exist even when these women are treated for these issues (King & Flenady, 2002). In fact, in a study by Goldenberg, Cliver, Mulvihill, Hickey, Hoffman, Howard, Klerman, & Johnson (1996), 46 risk factors were able to explain less than 10% of the variance in birth weight in babies born to White and Black women. What then accounts for these differences?

There are two destructive processes affecting the fetus. Dr. Michael Lu is the associate administrator of maternal and child health of the Health Resources and Services Administration (HRSA). I briefly met Dr. Lu at a lecture he conducted in Jacksonville. I was fascinated by his work on infant mortality and stress of the mother. About one destructive process, he and his co-author, Dr. Halfon, wrote, "Exposures and experiences during particularly sensitive developmental periods in early life may encode the functions of the organs or systems that become manifest in health and disease later in life" (Lu and Halfon, 2003, p. 6). According to Dr. Pathik Wadhwa, Assistant Professor of Behavioral Science, Obstetrics, and Gynecology at the University of Kentucky College of Medicine, the fetus responds to stimuli in the womb and adapts physiologically, which puts it at risk for several stress-related pathologies after birth (Fetus to mom: "You're stressing me out!, 2005). The disproportionately high rates of certain diseases in stressful communities are not only a result of poor eating and a lack of exercise, but the marker for poor health may be in some kids at birth. An infant girl may already be vulnerable to experiencing preterm labor, low birth rates, and other chronic health issues later in life.

Another destructive process is the impact of stress over a lifetime prior to pregnancy. Previous research on infant mortality seemed to assume that the lifelong chemical and psychological influence of stress could just simply be erased during nine months of pregnancy. When Black women do everything right for the nine months of pregnancy—including eating right, exercising, and managing stress—they are surprised that their rates of infant mortality are still higher. Experiencing traumatic stress throughout life increases the likelihood of creating what is essentially a war zone in the womb, adversely affecting the fetus. Talk about being counted out at the start!

SUMMARY

Chronic stress has proven catastrophic for Blacks in America. From birth to end of life, its effects have severely stunted the potential of a people whose physical toil disproportionately helped to build America. Maybe the most significant result of chronic stress has been its production of fear. While it is Whites who cite fear as the reason they shoot unarmed Blacks, most people, including Blacks themselves, don't understand that it is Blacks who live in a constant state of fear in America. Why would anyone in their right mind resign themselves to struggling to make ends meet or engaging in a criminal lifestyle that will surely lead to jail or death? It is easy for people to attribute the lack of competition against Whites to laziness, but it takes a lot of hard work to sustain an existence through working entry-level jobs. Some people don't work as hard as the people they hire to clean their houses. Petty criminals constantly have to duck other criminals and the police because of the possibility of getting hurt, killed, or jailed. They have to be on their toes constantly, amounting to much longer hours and harder work than the cushy desk jobs many of us enjoy.

What people don't understand is that these individuals have consciously or unconsciously made a calculation that this route would likely yield better results than competing with Whites. Many Blacks seem afraid of Whites. Black men in particular appear terrified. Many feel emasculated as evidenced in the music. Psychology 101 teaches us that people overcompensate for their insecurities. Common themes in hip-hop include making exorbitant amounts of money, having as many women as possible, having a large penis, and being tough enough to beat anyone in a fight. For some, this "uber-male" persona is merely a mask for feelings of insecurity, which is understandable given that Black men have been the targets of an unprecedented terror campaign in America. Emasculating Black men was a stated goal during slavery and has been subtly and not so subtly reinforced since that time. People forget that Black men were not only hanged, but often castrated. It wasn't that long ago that Black men had to call White little boys "sir," while their own kids looked on. Whites referred to Black men as boys, regardless of age. What goes on in the mind of a Black kid who has to watch his father be treated that way? What goes on in the mind of a White kid who sees this? How can both sets of kids not, at least subconsciously, think of Blacks as inferior and Whites as superior? Remember that a significant number of people who experienced and witnessed this kind of treatment are still alive today.

Youth in Baltimore rioted this year in response to the mysterious death of Freddie Gray while he was in police custody. I saw an interview one morning during the riots with a sharp young Black city council member, Brandon Scott. He was asked to comment on the looting that was taking place in the city. He suggested a major cause of the problem is the lack of male role models in that community. He went on to discuss the importance of role models. I agree with everything he said, but he missed the deeper issue, as did the reporters, unfortunately. They never followed up with a simple question to understand why there were so few male role models in that community. They missed a perfect opportunity to discuss how paralyzing fear has overcome the natural instinct for Black men to be strong, positive fathers, and role models in their communities. Many have opted, instead, for what they believe to be the easy way out—which has resulted in certain jail or an early death.

PART III

A NEW APPROACH TO INCLUSION

CHAPTER 6

Resilience Booster: The Unconventional Case for Reparations and Reconciliation

Injustice anywhere
is a threat to justice everywhere.
—Dr. Martin Luther King, Jr.

A new approach to igniting America's human resources is long overdue. The new approach would consist of an understanding of both the unparalleled prowess and the undeniable fragility of the human mind. The approach would merge the fields of education, sociology, psychology, neuroscience, and anthropology to apply the best of what researchers know about human development and human behavior to find the answers to overcoming racial issues that have eluded us to this point. Some of the specific recommendations I present in this chapter are new. Other ideas are not new but have not been implemented. Some of the ideas have been piloted but not brought to scale.

Reparations and reconciliation would help to erase America's tragic disparities and position the country to demonstrate to the rest of the world just how much of an advantage cultural diversity can offer. Like the term

"White privilege," the word "reparations" generally draws a damning emotional response from Whites. This reaction is particularly common among poor Whites, who feel overlooked, and wealthy Whites, who strongly believe that their merit has set them apart. The idea of reparations for Blacks can be traced back to Union General William T. Sherman in 1865, who issued Special Field Order No. 15. The order read:

> The islands from Charleston, south, the abandoned rice fields along the rivers   for thirty miles back from the sea, and the country bordering the St. Johns river,   Florida,   are   reserved   and set apart for the settlement of the negroes [sic] now   m a d e free by the acts of war and the proclamation of the President of the United   States [...] each family shall have a plot of not more than (40) acres of tillable ground, and when it borders on some water channel, with not more than 800 feet water front, in the possession of which land the military authorities will afford them protection, until such time as they can protect themselves, or until Congress shall regulate their title (Gates, 2013).

As a result of the order, over 40,000 free Blacks settled in 400,000 acres of land in Skidaway Island, Georgia. The land, along with the fact that Blacks could also borrow mules from the army, resulted in the famous "40 acres and a mule" reference. Just a few months after it was issued, however, Andrew Johnson overturned after he was sworn in as President after Lincoln's assassination, which was racially motivated. The assassin, John Wilkes Booth, had written in a letter, "This country was formed for the white, not for the black man," before he shot President Lincoln (Philadelphia Inquirer, 1865).

I am actually writing this book from Jacksonville, Florida, which would have been part of the land that was set-aside for Blacks. Imagine how different the story of race in America might be had Sherman's order stood. It is likely that the wealth gap between Black and White citizens would exist to a lesser degree. To acknowledge what happened is important, but to spend too much time thinking about what could have been is unproductive. At this point, to grant land or money would be too complicated. Many people would be unprepared to deal with a sudden influx of land or cash. Lottery winners and high profile athletes often end up broke, for instance, not because they are bad people, but because they frequently lack the skills, experience, and associated world view to effectively handle their newly acquired riches. If one thinks about the world a certain way and has a particular value system on Monday, none of that will automatically change if he or she wins the lottery on Tuesday.

There is something that can be done. First of all, the country has to decide to get serious about this issue. We have to realize that we are suffering as a nation. Secondly, we must concentrate on sustainable and scalable efforts based on science, not politics. Thirdly, we must accept that, although there is a role for the private sector, the government has to play a central role in the solution. I think Americans are caught up in the wrong debate—"big government vs. little government." Those terms don't make sense to me. I am more concerned with efficient and effective government. I also think anger is misplaced when they say, "Government can't get anything right." The problem is with elected officials, who make policy decisions that affect how he gets his job done. The fact is that without the government and Civil Rights legislation, things would be much worse for Blacks.

Blacks *and* Whites who have been adversely affected by our country's continuing battle over race don't need "hand-outs" for short-term appeasement, but rather a hand up. A bold, comprehensive approach that would change the story of race in our country forever would consist of: (1) a national diversity training course based on the neuroscience of diversity. This course should be available in-person and on-line at no charge for individuals in every community in America; (2) every Black person should have free access to a trained staff of mental health professionals to deal with the cumulative effect of overt and hidden racism and its associated stress. Whites who need counseling to be "de-radicalized" should also have free access to mental health professions; (3) America's education system needs to be reformed to feature Social and Emotional Learning (SEL) programs, particularly in poor communities. There also needs to be a shift in how Americans view education to immediate actions designed for more long-term benefits.

NATIONAL DIVERSITY AND INCLUSION TRAINING COURSE

Traditional diversity training leaves a lot to be desired. The mere mention of diversity training often makes people in organizations roll their eyes and squirm in their seats. They desperately search to fill their calendars with other responsibilities on days the training is offered. The typical response is, "We already had that. Why do we have to do it again?" Diversity practitioners counter by giving the training different names such as "cultural competence," but when people realize this is simply a code name for diversity training, they still react unfavorably. After working in human resources for as long as I have, I can understand why many people feel this way. The training has often been uncomfortable and unproductive at best, and difficult and destructive at worst. Diversity trainers are often well meaning—they are typically Progressively Proactive— but they are also frequently Misinformed or Uninformed. It is difficult for trainers to present information related to human differences objectively because they also have personal challenges when dealing with the issue.

Outside of the workplace, there are few opportunities for people to learn about issues related to diversity and inclusion. Churches have long been thought of as the most segregated communities in America, so they haven't been the place to learn about these issues. Diversity courses are rarely offered and hardly ever required in K-12 or even higher education. As I have already pointed out, our neighborhoods are still segregated, so there are not real opportunities there. There is virtually nowhere for people to go to learn about how to deal with racial issues. Even when these subjects come up, there is no common language or agreed upon framework from which to draw.

Churches, community centers, schools, sports venues, government buildings, non-profit facilities, and hospitals can all pitch in to offer space where the community can come together to learn about race, birthing a new level of understanding and intelligent discourse. Rather than anger, despair, or guilt, listeners could walk away feeling enlightened and empowered. For this to occur, the training has to be delivered in a radically different manner than it has up to this point. The information has to be presented in a fun, engaging way, which is possible to do even with the weight of the subject. To be effective, the training must adhere to the following guidelines:

- Emotional intelligence skills development should be at the heart of the training (no pun intended). Leading with data won't do. Individuals need to first develop the ability to calmly and rationally consider the new information they are going to be receiving, which might be contrary to what they have believed all of their lives. EI skills will not only help people better absorb the training, but these skills will also help them more effectively connect with others and make better decisions after the training.

- The training course must emphasize hidden biases and other lessons from various disciplines, some of which are presented in this book. The focus has to shift from labels, such as "good" and "bad," when describing people. Modern science helps identify the problems as "human" problems, which makes it easier for people to admit their shortcomings.

- The trainers must be presented in a manner that won't alienate White males. Researchers indicate that many White males don't consider themselves to have a culture, so when they hear talk of cultural issues, they tend to think of other groups. Some diversity trainers have perpetuated this fallacy by consciously or subconsciously presenting diversity as anything other than White or male. For instance, they often refer to "protected classes" as excluding White males, but civil rights laws address all races and both genders. In other words, a White person cannot be fired for being a White person, and a man cannot be fired for being a man, which means they are "protected." Consider other "protected" categories to which White males could potentially belong—veterans, people with disabilities, and people over 40 years old.

- The training must avoid trying to "fix" Whites, Christians, men, heterosexuals, and other majority groups. These groups are not the only ones struggling to understand and embrace diversity. There exists a fallacy that just because someone is born in a non-dominant group, they understand diversity. Not only do all groups have difficulty understanding other groups, they often struggle with the diversity within their own groups as well.

MENTAL HEALTH COUNSELING AND SUPPORT

For Blacks

A cadre of mental health professionals need to be trained and deployed to deal with the natural consequences of the Black experience, particularly complex trauma, PTSD, and persistent-TS. These professionals need to be culturally competent and skilled at understanding the impact of these issues as well as the major factors that contribute to resilience so that people can overcome these challenges. According to Steven Southwick and Dennis Charney, resiliency factors include: (1) possessing realistic optimism; (2) being able to face fear; (3) having a strong moral compass; (4) practicing religion and/or spirituality; (5) having adequate social support; (6) having access to resilient role models, (7) engaging in physical fitness; (8) practicing brain fitness; (9) possessing cognitive and emotional flexibility; and (10) having meaning and purpose in life (2012). Therapy could certainly help with factors 1, 2, 3, 4, 9 and 10. Mental health professionals could especially help with enhancing positive thinking and discouraging negative thinking, which is good practice for learning and enhancing optimism, an important factor for understanding diversity as I learned in my dissertation study. Black people could be recruited to go into this field to increase the likelihood that other Blacks would seek out the help they need. Such an effort to encourage Blacks to pursue these careers would have the added benefit of improving educational attainment and increasing employment levels for them.

For Whites

It is not only Blacks who have been damaged by individual, institutional, and structural racism. Whites have been at once perpetrators and victims. They, too, could benefit from working with mental health professionals to understand how they have been affected. I once had a young White woman visit me at my office after she heard me deliver a speech about many of the concepts in this book. Almost in tears, she explained to me that she had been exposed to a great deal of negative conditioning about race. Both of her parents were active members of an extremist group. She said that, over the years, she had frequently seen them in the traditional attire for the group and had listened to their hate-filled speech and ill-conceived notions about who was "naturally" superior and who was "naturally" inferior. She had come to see me because she was tired and did not want her kids exposed to that way of life, but she didn't know what to do. She wanted some advice about how she could be proactive in giving her kids opportunities to view the world differently. This young lady was very brave, but it was obvious that she was struggling with how people she loved so much could hate others to such a degree for something as simple as race. I am certain that counseling could have benefited her. Counseling might help some young people avoid the lure of such extremist groups in the first place.

EDUCATION REFORM

Traumatic Stress and the "Great Equalizer"

The so-called "Achievement Gap" has plagued American schools for decades with little appreciation for the impact of traumatic stress on students, parents, and teachers. While education is the most commonly cited solution to the widespread disparities that Blacks experience in America, the idea that education will be the "great equalizer" has a hole or two. Obviously, with a Bachelor's degree, two Master's degrees, and a Doctorate, I am a huge proponent of education. However, data suggests that education is a threshold factor, meaning that it is necessary but not sufficient for success in America, particularly if you are Black. As I showed in Chapter 3, at every level of educational attainment, Whites earn more than Blacks and have a lower unemployment rate.

Getting an education will not guarantee fair treatment, but without it chances of success are extremely slim. It is difficult for kids who have an unhealthy outlook on life to understand what education can do for them, especially when they know people who look like them who have degrees and are still struggling. Some kids decide, somewhat rationally, that if school is not likely going to meaningfully change their lives, why bother paying attention or even going to class? Sometimes teachers can make the difference in helping kids stay in school. It is true that quality teachers can do wonders with students, but we expect way too much from them if we think they can tackle complicated issues such as persistent-TS. Despite the considerable talents and dedication of many of our teachers, they are not trained to handle this psychological challenge. There is also very little help for teachers in the schools. The ratio of counselors to children in our schools is hundreds of students to a single counselor. Even then, the type of counseling that occurs is not likely to target the effects of persistent-TS. This has to change.

K-12

We will not be able to compete on the global stage without radically transforming how we think about the purpose of education. To do so requires a comprehensive review of the system, which begins with understanding its origins, continues with openly and honestly evaluating its current efficacy, and ends with building a sustainable model that meets the needs of a growing and diverse population. What has happened in America's schools is no accident. In fact, some theorists suggest that schools were originally designed to create and perpetuate socioeconomic inequalities (Pai & Adler, 2001). Pai and Adler argue, "Compensatory education was said to have perpetuated institutional racism (perhaps unintentionally) by teaching children to assimilate into the mainstream culture and abandon their own unique ethnic traits" (p. 71). I participated in an eye-opening exercise during my doctoral program at the University of North Florida that seemed to bolster this perspective. One of my professors, Dr. Pritchy Smith, asked the class to develop a new school system with the goal of creating and perpetuating a society of "haves" and "have-nots." Before giving us some time to complete the assignment, he urged us to think of ourselves as "mean as hell" and willing to do anything we thought we could get away with to ensure our desired outcome. Here is a partial list of the tactics we suggested:

- Keep the "haves" and "have-nots" separate to exaggerate the differences.

- Ensure that school funding is neighborhood-based (e.g. from property taxes), so that wealthy neighborhoods could have the best schools.

- Ensure that the leadership positions in both schools are held by "haves" and the support positions are held by "have-nots" so that each group would better understand the positions to which they should aspire.

- Ensure that textbooks reinforce the desired outcome.

- Deploy inexperienced, unqualified teachers to the "have-not" schools, especially in the technical subjects, and send the better teachers to the "have" schools.

When we finished sharing our thoughts about what we, "the meanest people in the world," would do to create and perpetuate a system of inequality in our schools, we could not come up with anything that has not happened in American schools. In so many ways, schools have failed to provide the pathway to the American Dream for all of its citizens. The core American ideology that served as a foundation for schools was based on a White Anglo-Saxon Protestant perspective (Pai & Adler, 2001). Many of the methods, textbooks, and teaching materials used in today's schools are still rooted in that traditional way of thinking. For example, I only learned about a handful of prominent Blacks in my history class. The lack of inclusion of the true contributions of Blacks in America has been detrimental for Blacks and Whites alike. Blacks feel denigrated and find it difficult to identify with the lessons taught, while Whites grow ignorant and disrespectful of the contributions of others in the development of the nation. Consider much of the information about early immigration I presented in this book. How is it that our kids are not learning this information in school? Clearly, history class needs to provide a full, honest review of the country's history, which would include the contributions of all of its citizens.

Social and Emotional Learning (SEL) would provide kids with the tools they need to handle the positive and negative aspects of America's history. SEL is essentially EI training for children. One of the baseline skills, for instance, is "impulse control." An early example of the power of this skill is the famous marshmallow test conducted in the 1960s by Stanford University researcher Walter Mischel. Considering some behavior he noticed with his daughter and her friends, he decided to test their ability to delay gratification. He brought kids into a room one at a time. Before leaving the room, he would give the kid one marshmallow and tell him or her if he or she resisted eating it, he would return with another. For some of the kids, the poor marshmallows did not have a chance. The other kids, however, did all they could to avoid eating the single marshmallow. The researcher separated the kids into two groups:

the "grabbers," who gave in, and the "waiters," who held on until his return. He found that four-year-olds who were able to delay gratification were better able to manage life's challenges as they got older. In high school, they had better test scores, more pro-social behaviors, and better relationships with teachers. As adults, they had on average higher-paying jobs, more stable family lives, and better health outcomes (The Stanford Marshmallow Study, 2008).

Organizations all over the country hire individuals like me to help their employees improve their EI skills. Why wouldn't these skills be prioritized in our K-12 system? Such skills would help kids believe in themselves and know what they bring to the table. They would be confident and assertive. They would be interested in blazing their own trail rather than succumbing to peer pressure. These skills could help kids be more self-actualized; able to set goals and do what is needed to achieve them. Kids would feel that they are in control of their success despite their environment. They would understand the potential consequences of bad decisions. They would understand that there is a whole world of possibilities. They would know that it does not matter where they are from, but rather, where they end up. Maybe most importantly, these skills would help kids connect better with each other, something necessary for individual and team success later in their lives. As Akers and Porter put it in *Your EQ skills: Got what it takes?* (2003), "As the global economy expands and the world shrinks, people with the ability to understand other people, and then interact with them so that each is able to achieve their goals, will be the success stories of the future" (p. 66). Employers rank the following as the top five most important skills required for the future workforce: (1) professionalism, (2) teamwork, (3) oral communication, (4) ethics and social responsibility, and (5) reading comprehension (Casner, Lotto & Barrington, 2006). In this social media dependent society, where are our young folks going to learn these skills unless sweeping changes are implemented in the K-12 curriculum?

A shift must also be made to a global, real-world curriculum. The technical areas like math and science are important, but they need to be reexamined to ensure that they are taught in ways that approximate what really happens at home and on the job. Math and science should be aimed at improving problem-solving skills as opposed to rote memorization. What if, instead of thinking of them as enemies, our kids could collaborate with kids in China or Africa to complete assignments over the Internet? What if our kids could graduate high school fluent in English and at least one other language? What if special effort was made to discover and promote each child's creative talent? What if study-abroad opportunities were available for everyone, not just those who could afford them? Every K-12 student should be required to participate in an extracurricular activity. The fees for these activities should be subsidized for those at or below the poverty line. The long-term benefits are immense. Researchers have long linked musical ability with math performance, for instance. Venezuela is changing the lives of thousands of poor kids through the Simon Bolivar National Youth Orchestra. Their program has been so successful that the country has been described as the future of classical music (El Sistema: Changing lives through Music, 2008).

Ironically, we get very little training in the most important activity in which each of us will ever participate—being a parent. This is another key area where schools can help. A handful of schools offer some training opportunities, but not to the degree that is required. So many of us learn about parenting based on how our parents raised us. I realize that we are born with some instinctual parenting skills, but science has uncovered so much about child development and human behavior that it is almost criminal for parents not to learn what they can before experiencing some of the poor results of trial-and-error. There is science, for instance, about different styles of discipline and long-term outcomes. Nutrition is another key area where parents are typically doing a woefully inadequate job. Consistent with SEL principles, an emphasis should be placed on skills like empathy to help kids understand and connect with others, particularly people of different backgrounds.

Higher Education

Make higher education transformational instead of transactional. In other words, college has to be more than job preparation. Higher education certainly changed my life. Given what I discussed in this book about growing up in East St. Louis, it is highly doubtful that I would have gained the experience to write this book if I had forgone college and focused on getting a job after high school. First, my maturation process would have been cut short. At Illinois, I learned to find an apartment, pay bills, buy groceries, vote, and make healthcare decisions. I learned that diversity was about more than just Black and White. I learned how to be a self-starter because nobody really cared if I showed up at class or not. I could have gotten a job near East St. Louis after high school and learned a few of these skills, but a college campus was an ideal environment for learning, with scholars, writers, artists, and political figures regularly visiting our campus.

There were also some added benefits for me. I felt safer at U of I than I ever did at home. We could walk around at night and not have to worry too much about any trouble—except for the locals who would terrorize the campus sometimes. My college apartment was the nicest place that I had ever lived up to that point. My whole life was enriched by the quality and variety of people I met while there. My college experience did not just prepare me for a job. My time away at school prepared me to negotiate the challenges and complexities of life. I have a real pet peeve with folks that say, "Well, college is not for everyone." I suppose I know that not every individual will go to college, but that statement can be paralyzing for kids who do not have a family history of going to college. This kind of thinking gives too many kids an excuse not to dream big. People say things like, "I did not go to college, and I turned out okay." They make comments like, "My uncle worked as a carpenter and now owns his own business; he never went to college." They will say, "Billy never went to college, and he is a millionaire now." It is not that these things do not happen, but anecdotal examples, or "outliers," are hardly relevant when they do not reflect what is happening overall. Getting a job is a necessary but not sufficient responsibility for the 21st century global citizen. A job is a short-term goal. Short-term thinking is what got the United States into so many of the aforementioned issues regarding race. Too many people are concerned with going to work and then going home to sit on the couch. Enormous amounts of potential are being sapped each evening watching reality television shows, or worse, sitting in a prison cell.

Studies have clearly shown that participants in prison education programs have recidivism rates considerably lower than those of non-participants (Maximum security education, 2007). Funding for these prisoner education programs were slashed during the 1990s, even though the cost of keeping a prisoner in prison for one year exceeds the cost of educating prisoners for one year by a 10 to 1 ratio (Granoff, 2005). This is an example of how emotions cloud issues. Eliminating these programs was spurred largely by the war-on-crime bandwagon on which so many politicians were pressured to jump onto in the 1980s and 1990s. According to Lisa Feldman of the Justice Policy Institute, "...'tough on crime' policies passed during the Clinton Administration's tenure resulted in the largest increases in federal and state prison inmates of any president in American history" (2001). President Clinton has recently expressed regret over such policies, particularly the "three strikes bill" (BBC News, 2015). Sometimes it is hard for me to decipher who the real criminals are. We lock up these folks, many of whom have mental health issues, and effectively deny them the opportunity to change their lives even though the data suggests that it costs taxpayers like you and me more in the short- and long-term to keep them there.

A few years ago, I saw a *60 Minutes* program about Bard College (Maximum security education, 2007). Bard is consistently ranked among the top liberal arts colleges in the United States. The show highlighted Bard's prison initiative that focused on providing liberal arts education to prisoners. Critics initially mocked the idea as a waste of time and money. The prisoners proved the critics wrong. It was not really the data they shared on the program that impressed me so much. The images were so refreshing. Picture tough inmates in prison jumpsuits standing in a huddle on the prison yard talking. The camera focused in on their conversation, and viewers are shocked to learn that these guys are talking about figures like Plato and Socrates. The professor said that she had to start the curriculum at a low level because most of these people had never cared about education. She was shocked, however, to discover that these men moved through the material at a more ferocious rate than her non-prison students. These men were so into the learning that they could not put down the books. They would use their considerable free time to read more than the required amount and do extra assignments. By 2013, Bard granted nearly 300 degrees to Bard Prison Initiative (BPI) participants and enrolled more than 700 students (Bard Prison Initiative, 2013). Among formally incarcerated Bard students, less than 4 percent have returned to prison (Bard Prison Initiative, 2013).

The "Funding" Question

At this point, you are probably wondering where the money will come from to pay for all of this. First of all, we are already paying a steep price, both in monetary resources on anti-poverty programs that have had mixed results, and in terms of human resources with the lives set-aside or even snuffed out in America's challenged communities. Think about all the pain and suffering that many have endured just to line the pockets of the despicable few who want to maintain the status quo.

For the short-term, regardless of what bold actions we take, we will have to continue to support safety-net programs that address urgent needs. People all over America, including an alarming number of kids, will go to sleep hungry tonight. Countless others don't know where they will sleep tomorrow. If we only focus on these urgent needs, however, we will never break this cycle. The strategies that I have outlined to get us out of this cycle will require a significant investment, and the major returns will be long-term. For America to execute a "war" on individual, institutional, and structural racism, both intended and unintended, we must shift our priorities. America currently spends about $16 billion on foreign aid each year to help struggling communities all over the world (Rutsch, 2015). Additionally, we spend more than $80 billion per year domestically to help people rebuild their lives after natural disasters (Plummer, 2013 April 29). How can anyone visit places like East St. Louis and not declare them "disaster" areas, particularly in light of the harmful chemicals that inhabit the air and soils of such communities? Resources reserved to respond to emergencies, both foreign and domestic, should be reallocated to deal with the problems in these traumatized communities. Does the fact that children are dying in the streets of America not constitute an emergency?

SUMMARY

There is a place for all Americans to get involved in changing the future of race in America. The change must start with understanding and being honest about how we got to this point. People must realize that self-reflection makes us stronger. Citizens must acquire a better understanding of the outright discrimination that still exists in America's structures and institutions. Most importantly, we have to get a handle on how people, both Black and White, are unconsciously contributing to our ongoing issues. Fairness, personal responsibility, hard work, and merit, are all terms that should be more than empty rhetoric or code-words used to fuel emotions and drive policies that promote the status quo, or even take us back to darker times in America's history. A blend of findings from anthropology, neuroscience, sociology, economics, psychology, biology, and old-fashioned common sense could be used in new ways to finally conquer one of America's greatest challenges—the racial divide. We know the brain exhibits plasticity, which means it can change. When cells in the brain are actively used, they change and become more effective in transmitting their messages, forming more connections with other cells. In other words, practicing appropriate responses to stimuli creates new networks within the brain that begin to make responding appropriately to stimuli easier over time. Just as individual's brain can be rewired, so too, can the collective brain of the nation.

CHAPTER 7

Your Brain on Diversity:
What Each of Us Can Do

The shortest and surest way
to live with honor in the world
is to be in reality what we would appear to be;
all human virtues increase and strengthen themselves
by the practice and experience of them.

—Socrates

WHAT CAN EACH OF US DO?

I am sure you spend some time every couple of years during the Olympics watching sports that you would never pay attention to otherwise. I never watch synchronized swimming, diving, figure skating, curling, or gymnastics other than to cheer for the USA. It is always astonishing to me that the individuals or teams that I think do the best job frequently receive mediocre scores. How can the judges get it so wrong? Clearly, even though we are looking at the same things, we are *seeing* something quite different. I notice obvious things. Did they fall? Did he smile? Did they look confident? Did her outfit look good? The judges see that stuff too, but they also notice dozens of technical nuances that my eyes have not been trained to pick up. They have either participated in these events or studied them all of their lives. They bring a level of connoisseurship, or expertise, to their work that doesn't just come out of the blue. The average person can tell when something obviously has gone horribly wrong, but our lack of experience and education regarding these sports render us virtually inept in distinguishing good performance from great performance, or fair performance from poor performance. Is that not true of most things in life? Hobbies like collecting require an uncommon level of expertise about whatever it is being collected. Trades like carpentry, welding, and plumbing cannot be picked up overnight. How many of us can show up at our spouse's job and perform as well as she or he does? To effectively argue a legal case, prescribe the appropriate medication, or make a blueprint is going to take more than just watching actors playing lawyers, doctors, and engineers on television. Why, then, do we expect people to naturally connect across something as loaded as racial lines without education and experience?

We like to believe that people will just pick up these skills if they are smart, fair, and well meaning—you know—"good people." We could not be more wrong. Just as I have little idea of what to look for in a gymnast's floor routine, the average person lacks the skills to understand the subtle but relevant cultural differences they encounter in everyday life. Sure, we can catch the obvious differences like appearance, food, and language, but in this segregated society, we struggle to get the necessary experience to truly understand each other. Intra-group diversity adds to the complexity. Experience with one Black person tells us little about Black people. Experience with one Muslim tells us little about Muslims. Experience with one woman tells us little about women. Experience with one transgendered person tells us little about transgendered people. Just as one has to immerse him or herself in a new trade, profession, or hobby, it is only through multiple experiences that one can grow to recognize and appreciate relevant cultural differences. In other words, we must all become what I call "cultural connoisseurs."

Milton Bennett provides a process for becoming such a connoisseur in his Developmental Model of Intercultural Sensitivity (DMIS) (Bennett, 2000). Bennett's model is a continuum that begins with several "Ethnocentric" stages and moves to various "Ethnorelative" stages.

Bennett defined "ethnocentric" as consciously or subconsciously using one's own set of standards and customs to judge all people. The early ethnocentric stages of Bennett's model deal with the conscious stuff—negative, mean-spirited behavior, and outright discrimination. Individuals whose developmental level is in the earliest stages in Bennett's model may view members of the non-dominant groups who do not conform to the dominant culture as "stupid, depraved, irresponsible, psychopathic, inferior, or sinful to a point beyond all redemption" (Pai & Adler, 2001, p. 35). As I have indicated throughout the book, I don't believe most Americans hold these types of beliefs, at least not at a conscious level. The real area of opportunity for America is with people in the dominant and non-dominant groups who subconsciously perpetuate these beliefs.

There is a tendency for people to think that not actively discriminating against anyone is good enough. Others hope that if they avoid talking about cultural differences such as race, gender, and sexuality, the problems will go away. Bennett calls this stage "minimization." In other words, people at this stage try to minimize cultural differences while focusing on similarities among groups. Many people in the Dominant culture at this stage unknowingly enjoy the benefits of cultural congruence. They do not realize that they have tangible and psychological advantages of being in the dominant culture, so they fail to see the need to focus on strategies to "level the playing field." Some Dominant group members have never even thought about the fact that they are part of the dominant culture. When I am speaking to large groups, for instance, I often ask audience members to tell me the name of the last Black movie they saw. Some people scream out the latest Tyler Perry movie. I follow up that question by asking what the last White movie was that they saw was, and they look confused. Many Whites view movies with predominantly Black casts as Black movies, and few of them go to see them. On the other hand, movies with predominantly White casts are considered "regular" movies, and it is assumed that everyone would go to see them. Interestingly, because of the demographic makeup of America, not every White person needs to go to see movies with predominately White casts for the movies to do well. This is not true for movies or television shows with predominately Black casts. Television shows with predominantly Black casts seldom last very long. The networks are sometimes accused of being racist, but that isn't necessarily true. Cutting these shows might really boil down to business decisions. Many viewers watch shows that reflect their own cultures. If every Black household watched a show with a Black cast, there still might not be enough viewers to keep the show on television. On the other hand, with their numbers, White households can support several shows with predominately White casts even if they come on television at the same time. So is it really a racist conspiracy that there are few Black-themed shows on television? Should TV executives produce the Black shows anyway and lose money? There is another alternative, of course. If the networks were successful in drawing crossover audiences, the shows could be profitable and help move the country closer to understanding each other at the same time. Such movement could only occur if the shows explored Black themes as opposed to fitting Black people into storylines reflective of the experiences of White people.

Though it has been criticized for years, the "melting pot" idea still exists. Many Americans boast that our doors have historically been open to anybody who wanted to come and work for the American Dream. The primary criticism of this perspective is that in a society where there is a dominant racial group, pressure is exerted on individuals outside of that dominant group for them to assimilate rather than integrate. According to Pai and Adler, "What the melting pot myth did was reinforce the ethnocentrism of the majority and convince ethnic minorities that their ethnicity and cultural heritage were illegitimate and hence needed to be abandoned" (Pai & Adler, 2001, p. 63). Remember that having a Black-sounding name greatly decreased the likelihood that an applicant would be called back in the study I cited, regardless of education and experience. Many Jewish and Asian Americans responded to this pressure by ditching their original names. There are countless other examples of name changes, plastic surgeries, and voice lessons designed to "Americanize" or "Whiten" people, not to mention the fading creams and hair chemicals that Black people have tried over the years.

Become a Cultural Connoisseur

Think about being at a restaurant and observing the sommelier interact with a customer who is a wine connoisseur. If you are like most people, you understand little about the ritual they conduct. Wine experts are amazing in their abilities to discern subtle differences in wines, but they didn't acquire those skills overnight. As with anything else, wine expertise can be viewed through a continuum. At one end of the spectrum, there are nondrinkers who could not care less about wine. The cultural parallel would be people who have no interest in learning about cultural differences. As we move along the continuum, there are people who have tried wine, but didn't like the taste or how it made them feel. This parallels someone who has had a bad experience with a person from a different cultural group, so they avoid further interaction with people from that group.

Still in the initial stages on the wine continuum, people have very little ability to distinguish among varieties of wine. They group all wine together, or put them into broad categories, such as "white wines" and "red wines." One red wine to these people represents all red wines. The cultural equivalent would be grouping together all Asians or all Latinos. Just as one's palate is unable to understand differences in the taste and texture of red wines at this point, the cultural palate is unable to understand the differences between the many and varied Asian cultures. The "Law of the Subgroup" emerges. If I hired twenty people to work for me and the numbers were proportional to the population (which they are not in many cases), 16 would be White, two would be Black and two would be Hispanic. Anything negative that the Black or Hispanic person did would mean that 50% of that group performed poorly. Even if seven White people performed poorly, that is less than 50%, so the overall impression of the group would not likely be as negative. Think again about the television show example. It is difficult to keep a show with a predominantly Black cast since only 13.2% of the population is Black, but consider the damage that one terrible Black show could cause (U.S. Census Bureau, n.d.). For every bad Black show, there could be dozens of bad White shows before the issue of harmful White shows became evident.

Moving along the connoisseurship continuum, people discover that not only are there red and white wines, but there are different varieties within each group. There are, in fact, over 50 varieties of fine wine grapes including Barbera, Brunello, Cabernet Franc, Cabernet Sauvignon, Carignane, Carmenere, Cinsault, Dolcetto, Durif, Gamay, Grenache, Grignolino, Malbec, Merlot, Montepulciano, Nebbiolo, Petit Sirah, Petit Verdot, Pinotage, Pinot Meunier, Pinot Noir, Sangiovese, Syrah/Shiraz, Tempranillo, Tinta Barroca, Tinta Cao, Touriga Francesa, Touriga Nacional, Tinta Roriz, and Zinfandel; these are just the red grape varieties (Wine grape varieties, n.d.). Similarly, instead of grouping people together into broad categories like "foreigner," or using "Chinese" to describe anyone from Asia, people at this stage soon recognize just how diverse groups are. On this planet, there are many ethnic Asians: Ainu, Alorese, Azerbaijani, Bhote, Bihari, Burmese, Burusho, Buyi, Chamorro, Chukchee, Erh-li-t'ou, Filipino, Gilyak, Gurungs, Han, Hmong, Hun, Iban, Ifugao, Japanese, Jomon, Kapauku, Khalka Mongols, Korean, Lao Loum, Lao Soung, Liangzhu, Lolo, Malay, Manchu, Mbau Fijians, Miao, Nicobarese, Pentecost, Rhade, Siamese, Sinhalese, Tabon Caves, Uygur, Vietnamese, Wanniyalaeto, and Yapese (Asian cultures, n.d.). Many people at this stage may recognize that there are differences within these broad categories, but they might still be tempted to minimize the differences because they do not understand them. Others might be excited about all the learning that awaits them on this journey to connoisseurship.

Further along the continuum, people learn of the different wine and food combinations. They start taking risks and becoming more adventurous in experiencing different wines. While they cannot quite articulate the differences in wine varieties to any specificity, they can distinctly taste differences. They start to understand what they like and don't like. This is like moving into Bennett's ethnorelative half of the IDI. In other words, context matters. People realize that their own cultural viewpoint may not be appropriate for every situation, so they begin to attend certain cultural functions that might be outside of their comfort zone. Over time, they do not just go to watch, but also to participate and experience the differences between a Black Baptist Church and a Bahai Temple, for instance. These experiences, rather than spark the formation of stereotypes from afar, offer a close-up view of the various nuances among cultural groups. People along this cultural journey realize that the goal is not to compare and declare one culture better or worse than another, but to understand and appreciate the differences. People continue on this trajectory until they become connoisseurs. They become like the Olympic judges. Wine experts develop a palate to detect the subtle nuances in the sweetness, saltiness, acidity, and bitterness of wines. Not only are they more literate about different varieties of wines, their experience with wine is much more fulfilling at each successive step along the continuum, which can also happen as people experience different cultures. So, just as any wine expert goes through this process where he or she develops an in-depth understanding about the nuances of their subject matter, one can gain such expertise about cultural differences. At this point, not only do they recognize and enjoy experiencing these subtle differences, but they can also adjust their behavior to operate effectively in different environments. They have become cultural connoisseurs.

Beware of the Promises and Perils of Culture

There is something magical about culture and tradition. For many, connecting to the past provides a kind of cathartic experience. Learning is often passed down through generations and, in some communities, daily survival depends on this learning. Culture and tradition also provides a vehicle for individuals to bond with others and express themselves. For all the richness and promise of culture, it also comes with great peril. People all over the world continue the rituals, customs, and practices that are physically and mentally harmful only because their ancestors have done things that way for centuries. People continue to engage in dangerous rites of passage, eat and drink foods that cause chronic disease, and take pride in self-destructive behaviors in an attempt to fit into certain groups. Individuals often view legendary figures from their culture through revisionist lenses. In other words, they take great pride in the positive characteristics of their historic figures while ignoring any negative attributes.

To overcome the traps that rob their individual and collective development, every ritual, custom, and practice that is common to the cultural groups with which they identify, such as race, religion, nationality, gender, sexuality, or any of the dozens of other items I could list, need to be carefully examined. Some of these practices and behaviors form the basis for the negative, hurtful stereotypes at the heart the conflicts between cultures. After deep reflection and introspection, people should abandon the customs and traditions that are damaging to themselves or others, such as Native American mascots, and hold on to the ones that help advance individuals in that group, and by extension, society as a whole. With serious issues looming such as America's obesity epidemic, domestic and foreign terrorism, the growing wealth gap, and human trafficking, how can people get so emotionally invested in something like a mascot? If we have any hope of helping America fulfill its enormous potential, we have got to be deeper than that. U of I could adopt a light bulb as the mascot and it won't change my feelings about the school one bit. Our academic and athletic records and accomplishments don't change. Culture and tradition cannot continue to be a barrier to personal and professional growth and progress, individually or as a nation.

WHAT ELSE CAN WHITE AMERICANS DO?

Whites need to be able to differentiate among Blacks as they do among Whites. When a White person does something ridiculous on the national stage, unless the issue is about race, Whites feel no responsibility for those actions. The small business owner who told me that White people who had performed poorly for her were "White trash," not "regular" White people, expressed this sentiment. Whites cross to the other side of the street when they see certain Whites walking towards them. There are White people that other Whites would never hire, date, or trust with their kids. Yet, many Whites seem to view race as the primary characteristic they need to know when it comes to Blacks. This fact was demonstrated in the "What's in a Name" study where Black-sounding names from Ivy League schools got no more favorable response from perspective employers than Black-sounding names from less prestigious schools, which was not the case for White sounding-names from more prestigious schools. To treat a professionally dressed Black person in the same manner as a Black person dressed unprofessionally, but treat a professionally dressed White person with more respect than an unprofessionally dressed White person is problematic. The fact is that everyone should be respected regardless of attire, but in reality, we make those distinctions within our own race every day. We should be able to make them across racial lines.

WHAT ELSE CAN BLACK AMERICANS DO?

Offer Alternatives to Explicit Hip-Hop and Its Associated Culture

There has long been a debate in America about the influence of hip-hop music. The degree to which hip-hop defines Black culture is arguable, but there is no denying its widespread popularity. The music is ubiquitous, and Whites are the largest consumer group. Predominantly White ballet studios across America offer hip-hop dance lessons. Those who feel hip-hop music is a negative force refer to the broken English, foul language, misogyny, references to violence and substance abuse. They point out the tattooed, platinum-toothed young men prancing around with their pants hanging below their butts wearing tank tops commonly referred to as "wife-beaters." Critics also point out that not only does the music depict a negative and destructive lifestyle, but these guys often find themselves in trouble with the law for the very crimes they rap about, which is evidence that what we hear in their lyrics is hardly make-believe.

Hip-hop artists capitalize on the sense of resentment that some Black youth have about being born into such dire circumstances. To cope with this anger, they try to make a negative into a positive. As such, they claim growing up in the "hood" is a badge of honor. They reject anything that seems "White." They try hard not to speak "standard" English. They use the term "nigga" regularly as a term of endearment. Women in these communities often see the men as meal tickets, and the men view the women as objects—"bitches" and "hoes." Crime and disobedience are just a part of life for them. Their world has different rules. They have made a conscious decision not to be victims by doing the victimizing themselves. Mahatma Gandhi describes this phenomena in terms of "active vs. passive" violence. According to Gandhi's grandson Arun, who co-founded The M.K. Gandhi Institute for Nonviolence, "we are conditioned to look at violence only in its physical manifestation -- wars, fighting, killing, beating, rapes -- where we use physical force. We don't, however, consider oppression in all its forms -- name-calling, teasing, insulting, disrespectful behavior -- as passive forms of violence (Gandhi, n.d.). Gandhi made the point that passive violence leads to active violence because people who have been oppressed have not been taught an effective way of dealing with the resulting anger. It should be no surprise that some of them unleash that anger on the most convenient targets, people in their communities. Individuals who engage in this behavior appear on the surface to have a high self-regard, but it is often a mask to cover anger, fear, and insecurity. Despite their hard exterior, many of them are afraid to compete with Whites because they know they have not been properly prepared. Young hip-hop artists and the growing cadre of self-proclaimed R&B "thugs" reinforce these behaviors through the glorification of this lifestyle.

Today, I agree with the critics who admonish rappers for their brand of entertainment, but I would not have agreed when I was in my teens and early 20s. In the 1980s and early 1990s, hip-hop was mostly positive and fun. I enjoyed the "positive" artists, but the real attraction for me and just about everybody I knew were the groups that were too explicit for the radio. What appealed to me most then was West Coast rap, which described life as I knew it in East St. Louis. Though the geography was different, I felt theses artists were representative of my struggles and me. They understood me, which was empowering. When I now listen to some of the stuff I enjoyed the most in high school and college, I cringe. The glamorization of violence and objectification of women in the music cannot be denied. On the other hand, the immense talent of many of the artists was clearly evident. The vivid imagery, concise storytelling, and catchy hooks captured the attention of kids all over America and ire of their parents. The lure of this rebellious music is typical teenage behavior. Every generation has felt that the music to which their kids were listening was some sort of sign of the apocalypse. According to Howard (2006), "Adolescence [is] the period characterized by major brain growth, hormonal changes, physical changes, emotional changes and social changes" (pp. 94–95). The excess capacity in the brain, strong hormonal urges to explore new things, and elevated levels of dopamine (which stimulates curiosity, fantasizing, and risk-taking) make teenagers destined to challenge rules (Howard, 2006). Their motivation is aimed at short-term pleasures because the instrument responsible for long-term planning and execution, the prefrontal cortex, is yet to be fully developed.

I have since erased all music from my collection that has explicit language, offensive references to women, glorification of violence, or positive references to drugs. I cannot as a responsible adult promote such messages, and I certainly won't let my kids listen to such things. When I happen to hear any new hip-hop, I am saddened that it seems to be getting worse. Maybe what upsets me is the fact that the music has become so mainstream that the behaviors have been accepted as just typical Black male behavior. Money, guns, marijuana, and strippers seem to be the winning formula for each hip-hop hit. I am not sure how anyone can deny that the music negatively affects the behavior of some of its listeners. Go to a local high school and look at how people dress. Go to a local nightclub and observe what drinks people order, and then get in the car, turn on the radio and count how many references to that same drink you hear. Hip-hop music is where many young people learn about drugs and guns. Boys, many of whom grow up without male role models in their homes, learn about how to treat women from hip-hop artists. The message of getting as much money as possible as quickly as possible resonates with many young people who later find themselves in jail trying to live the life they hear about in the music. Hip-hop artists argue that they don't create the situations they rap about, but rather inform us of what is happening. I agreed with that 25 years ago, but we know what's happening today. We get it! They also argue that rap music has catapulted so many individuals from abject poverty and certain prison or death to abundant success. I am glad for those people, but why would they turn around and lead people down the same path? The influencing power of hip-hop is no different from the influencing power of other rebellious music that has been worshipped by kids who have committed school shootings in the United States. The messages in the music serve as a form of what I call neuro-manipulation—the exploitation of a vulnerable population.

I have come to believe that it would be impossible to stop young people from making this kind of music. It is within the design of their brains to test the boundaries. I also realize that I am foolish to believe that poor kids who are offered lucrative contracts to make this kind of music would turn down those deals to take a moral stand. Think about the highly educated CEOs and politicians who are in jail today because of greed, or the ones exploiting consumers every day for profit. Whether it is Black kids making hip-hop, White kids making silly reality shows,

Hollywood making violent movies, or video game manufacturers making violent games, I know that I can't stop this lucrative runaway locomotive, especially given the rise of social media.

The problem is that, unlike White kids, Black kids don't perceive many options for themselves other than listening to this type of music and embracing this type of culture. Like I felt at their age, they feel this music represents them. Research indicates that the peer group influence is greatest between ages of eight and twenty-five. While kids are members of multiple peer groups, remember that it is the salient peer group with which the kid most identifies. Youngsters adopt the rules and norms of this salient peer group and do anything they can to minimize the differences between themselves and the group. They also develop hostility toward members of other groups, which gets them even more ideologically entrenched in their chosen peer group. In *The Tipping Point* (2000), Malcolm Gladwell provides numerous provocative examples of the powerful influence of the salient peer group. For example, Gladwell wrote about the rash of suicides that occurred in Micronesia in the 1970s and 1980s. The more these unspeakable acts gained the public's attention, the more they became a "ritual of adolescence" (Gladwell, 2000, p. 218). The suicide victims generally fit the same profile and followed the same protocols for hanging themselves. Similarly, from 2007 to 2012, 79 people killed themselves in Brigend, South Wales. The high number of copycat suicides prompted the police to ask the media to stop covering them (The Telegraph, 2008). I think a similar thing is happening in our urban communities in America—not with suicide, but with violent crimes. It seems the intense media coverage of the "problems" with young Black males, coupled with the apparent glorification of these types of crimes through music, worsens the situation. Is it really so hard to believe that hearing about a violent crime in a song will make some kids more prone to commit violent crimes when we have clear examples of copycat suicides influenced by media coverage?

My greatest disappointment is with the current and former adult hip-hop artists, many of whom have become very successful business people. Just as I have matured and changed my worldview as a result of being exposed to people and places beyond East St. Louis, I have to believe they feel differently about the world today than they did as kids. They see very clearly now that the odds are slim that hoards of aspiring young rappers are going to make it to their level. They have to know also that the behaviors promoted in much of the genre will lead to a jail cell or a casket. These icons no longer need street credit, so they have nothing to lose. They should use their considerable resources to create different paths to success for young people. I am not saying they have to deny or even regret things they did in their past. Power, influence, employee relations, customer service, marketing, sales, and distribution are skills they honed on the streets. Sudhir Venkatesh learned about this firsthand when he lived with a notorious Chicago street gang for seven years while working on his doctorate (Researcher studies gangs by leading one, 2008). Venkatesh learned about the complex organizational structure of the gang, its detailed record-keeping procedures, and the impressive management skills of its leader. Why can't these successful guys say, "I did what I had to do so that you don't have to do what I did." While I know teens are designed to like the edgy stuff, it is hard for me to believe that well-produced tracks about education, positive family life, good health, and career success wouldn't sell if the hooks were catchy and the right artists delivered the lyrics.

Black folks have to aim higher. To be excessively influenced by others, such as hip-hop artists, pop singers, reality show contestants, entertainers, athletes, or other so-called celebrities in order to justify a cultural connection is foolish. We have to know that giving our kids names that the parents can barely pronounce is not going to be good for those kids. We have to know that we are likely never going to have jobs leading to promising careers with purple hair and tattoos all over our bodies. That doesn't even work for Whites. You may be smart, kind, and hardworking, but you are simply not going to be taken seriously unless you present a professional image, particularly if you are Black. Why present yourself in a manner that you know will elicit certain types of reactions unless you really want those reactions?

Adopt a Culture of Entrepreneurship

The critical racial problem in America is the wealth gap. Wealth changes everything. The achievement gap between Black kids and White kids, for example, all but disappears when controlling for wealth. An untapped avenue to achieving generational wealth in America for Blacks is ownership of a successful business. There should be a major marketing campaign aimed at inspiring young people to become entrepreneurs with resources available to help them be successful.

1. Wealthy Blacks could develop a national endowment that would provide startup capital for promising Black-owned businesses. Books and other materials could be sold with the proceeds going to the fund.

2. The fund could sponsor statewide entrepreneurship contests at the high school level throughout the country.

3. Rather than just barber shops and hair salons, emphasis should be placed on establishing businesses that would attract a broader population of customers than only Black people. Health and wellness could be a great area of opportunity. Americans of all backgrounds are struggling with obesity and associated chronic health issues, and across the board the numbers for Blacks are worse than for Whites. Health food stores, healthy restaurants, and fitness centers could be successful anywhere with the added benefit having a dramatic impact in poor communities.

4. The fund could establish entrepreneur programs at each Historically Black College and University (HBCU) that doesn't currently have such programs.

GET HEALTHY!

There may be no better way to demonstrate self-respect than taking care of your health. America is in the midst of a health epidemic. Over two-thirds of Americans are overweight, and a third of those who are overweight are obese (Ogden, Carroll, Kit, & Flegal, 2012). Half of all adults have one or more chronic health conditions. One in four adults have two or more chronic health conditions (CDC, n.d.). These diseases are the most costly in term of lives and dollars, yet they are the easiest to prevent. All groups of Americans need to change their behavior regarding exercise and nutrition, but like so many areas, Blacks suffer from these conditions disproportionately. For instance, obesity rates are high among Blacks – 38.8% of men and 58.5% of women are obese, compared to 36.2% and 32.2% of Whites, respectively (Ogden et.al., 2012). Combating obesity is not about vanity—it's about quality of life.

Aerobic exercise and weight training are essential for proper brain functioning as well, according to a review of more than 100 recent studies by exercise scientists at my Alma Mater, The University of Illinois. Just a few of the brain benefits of exercise include improving memory, lengthening attention span, and improving multitasking and planning skills. Most people understand the importance of exercise, but they underestimate the importance of nutrition. Described as the most comprehensive dietary and lifestyle study ever conducted, "The China Study" looked at the relationship between people, their environment, and their food choices. It examined the eating habits of residents living in over 60 counties in rural China. The researchers noted that rural Chinese diets were largely composed of plant-based foods while the diets of Chinese people living in more affluent areas included more meat (money was a factor). The researchers concluded that a plant-based diet dramatically decreased the risk of cancer, cardiovascular disease, diabetes, and obesity (Campbell and Campbell, 2004). My family has practiced a whole foods plant-based diet for six years now. We were vegetarians over three years before that, so it's been nearly a decade since we have eaten meat or dairy.

Such a lifestyle would certainly be more challenging in America's "food deserts," but entirely doable. The law of supply and demand dictates that if people begin to demand fresh, healthy foods, smart business people will find a way to provide those items. It is true that access has been part of the problem, but culture has been the major hurdle.

SUMMARY

Americans like to talk about personal responsibility. There is an opportunity for Whites and Blacks to demonstrate personal responsibility to become Progressively Proactive and change America's race story. Whites have a significant responsibility to become educated about these issues and recognizing structural, institutional, and individual bias. Blacks, particularly successful Blacks, have to realize that such treatment has had a major impact on the collective psyche of the Black Community. By helping to usher in an error of entrepreneurship for Blacks, these individuals can inspire extraordinary personal and professional success in communities that are today crippled. Both Whites and Blacks can become "cultural connoisseurs," which will make connecting across racial lines easier and much more interesting.

There is also a role for government. The message has to be clear that America wants its whole team on the field and is willing to invest time and treasure to make it happen. The private sector can help with funding for the diversity training and counseling. The non-profit sector can help by adopting the strategies in this book to help them to carry out their individual missions. Elected officials need to be courageous and fact-driven instead of caving to the desires of Regressively Reactive and Regressively Proactive voters. Schools have the significant role of preparing students to successfully navigate an increasingly diverse world. The curriculum and format has to change to ensure that this happens.

If we don't pull together to make this country work for all of us, 50 years from now, there will be an author whose book will start similar to this one with: "This year, America celebrated the 100th anniversary of the most significant piece of Civil Rights legislation in its history, the Voting Rights Act of 1965, prohibiting racial discrimination in voting, but Black Americans are still struggling."

AFTERWORD

In Search of a Transformational Leader

A leader is responsible for establishing a vision and the developing collective goals. A leader is also responsible for generating and maintaining enthusiasm, confidence, optimism, cooperation, and trust (George, 2000). I cannot stress enough the importance of optimism. The theory of positive emotions suggests that, "Positive emotions broaden the scope of attention, expand and open the individual's mind to new types of information, enhance cognitive flexibility, and increase the capacity to form creative and meaningful connections" (Southwick & Charney, 2012). Citizens must begin to hold politicians accountable to be effective leaders. The populous must elect leaders who have demonstrated their ability to relate to and work on behalf of the people culturally different from themselves—they must be cultural connoisseurs. Wealth should not be a factor in determining who should govern the country. Besides the influence of money, the worst part about America's political system is that politicians won't tell their constituents when they are wrong. Sometimes the facts don't line up with people's individual experiences and beliefs, and politicians know it but lack the moral courage to do something about it. These future political leaders will have to be courageous enough to stand up to their constituents and educate them as opposed to just following their emotional whims.

Outside of politics, the country is poised for a transformational leader to spark a movement to directly confront the most open secret in American history—the pitting of working class Whites against Blacks through neuro-manipulation. This revolution must be fueled not by armament, but by courage and wisdom. I believe he or she is out there. She may be an infant in her mother's arms trying to make sense of the world. He may be a young kid trying to figure out why some people are treated different from others, or a teenager struggling to understand our hang-ups about skin color. She may be a college student just learning about some of the unspeakable acts of terror Americans have committed against other Americans, or a worker frustrated with the constant racial divisiveness of the public sphere. He might even be a retiree who has lived through some ugly times in the 1950s and 1960s and doesn't want his great grandkids to have to experience these issues.

Maybe there are two leaders out there—one Black and one White. Each would need to be an effective role model for individuals who look like them, but also possess enough charisma, empathy, and authenticity to connect with and inspire people who don't. This powerful tandem could demonstrate what can be accomplished when people work together across racial lines.

Maybe one of these great leaders has just finished reading this book.

References

Preface

Augustine, M. (2013, October 17). In his own words: Prison letters from Michael Dunn. *WOKV News*. Retrieved from http://www.wokv.com/news/news/local/his-own-words-prison-letters-michael-dunn/nbQkg/

Federal Bureau of Investigation (2013). Hate crime statistics, 2012. Retrieved from http://www.fbi.gov/about-us/cjis/ucr/hate-crime/2012/topic-pages/incidents-and-offenses/incidentsandoffenses_final

Gabrielson, R., Jones, R. G., & Sagara, E. (2014, October 10). Deadly force, in black and white: A ProPublica analysis of killings by police shows outsize risk for young black males. *ProPublica*. Retrieved from http://www.propublica.org/article/deadly-force-in-black-andwhite?utm_source=et&utm_medium= email&utm_campaign=-dailynewsletter

Go deeper: Where race lives (n.d.). In *Race: The power of an illusion*. Retrieved from http://www.pbs.org/race/000_About/002_06-godeeper.htm

Hate incidents. (n.d.). Southern Poverty Law Center. Retrieved from http://www.splcenter.org/get-informed/hate-incidents

Hernandez, S. (2015, May 7). Two San Francisco police officers resign, six more face firing over racist texts. *BuzzFeed News*. Retrieved from http://www.buzzfeed.com/salvadorhernandez/racist-texts-between-san-francisco-cops-spark-review-of-3000#.jtXd195DRo

Lovett, I. (2013, August 21). In California, a champion for police cameras. *New York Times.* Retrieved from http://www.nytimes. com/2013/08/22/us/in-california-a-champion-for-police-cameras. html?_r=0

Observations concerning the increase of mankind, peopling of countries, etc. (n.d.). Retrieved from http://www.columbia.edu/~lmg21/ ash3002y/earlyac99/documents/observations.html

Potok, M. (2014). The year in hate and extremism. *Intelligence Report,* (153). Retrieved from http://www.splcenter.org/get-informed/intelligence-report/browse-all-issues/2014/spring/The-Year-in-Hate-and-Extremism

Shapiro, E. (2015, May 14). Racist, homophobic texts revealed between San Francisco police officers. *ABC News.* Retrieved from http://abcnews.go.com/US/racist-homophobic-texts-revealed-san-francisco-police-officers/story?id=29638149

Southwick, S. M., & Charney, D. S. (2012). *Resilience: The science of mastering life's greatest challenges.* New York: Cambridge University Press.U.S. Department of Justice. (2015, April 5). *Investigation of the Ferguson Police Department.* Washington, DC: U.S. Government Printing Office.

Van Derbeken, J. (2015, March 16). Bigoted texts 'disgraced' SFPD, chief says, vowing rapid action. Retrieved from http://www.sfgate. com/crime/article/Officers-linked-to-racist-texts-were-all-veterans-6134489.php

Williams, T. (2015, April 3). San Francisco police officers to be dismissed over racist texts. *New York Times.* Retrieved from http://www. nytimes.com/2015/04/04/us/san-francisco-police-officers-to-be-dismissed-over-racist-texts.html

Zavadski, K. (2015, June 20). Everything known about Charleston Church shooting suspect Dylann Roof. *The Daily Beast.* Retrieved from http://www.thedailybeast.com/articles/2015/06/18/everything-known-about-charleston-church-shooting-suspect-dylann-roof.html

Introduction

Childress, S. (2014, October 20). Why voter ID laws aren't really about fraud. *Frontline*. Retrieved from http://www.pbs.org/wgbh/pages/frontline/government-elections-politics/why-voter-id-laws-arent-really-about-fraud/

McElwee, S. (2015, March 9). Millennials are more racist than they think. *Politico*. Retrieved from http://www.politico.com/magazine/story/2015/03/millenials-race-115909.html#.VUgp50sujmI

Pew Research Center (2010, February 24). Millennials: Confident. Connected. Open to change. Retrieved from http://www.pewsocialtrends.org/2010/02/24/millennials-confident-connected-open-to-change/

Shelby County, Alabama v. Holder, Attorney General, et. al., 570 U. S. (2013). Retrieved from http://www.supremecourt.gov/opinions/12pdf/12-96_6k47.pdf

United States Department of Justice (n.d.). Section 5 of the Voting Rights Act. Retrieved from http://www.justice.gov/crt/about/vot/sec_5/about.php

Chapter 1

Asmerom, R. (2010, September 27). Why do Koreans own the black beauty supply business? *Madame Noire*. Retrieved from http://madamenoire.com/104753/why-do-koreans-own-the-black-beauty-supply-business/

Cummins, S., & Macintyre, S. (2002). "Food deserts" evidence and assumption in health policy making. *British Medical Journal*, 325, 436–438.

East St. Louis, Illinois. (n.d.). Retrieved from http://www.city-data.com/city/East-St.-Louis-Illinois.html#ixzz3ZEE91qGN

Federal Bureau of Investigation. (n.d.). Crime in the United States, 2012. Retrieved from http://www.fbi.gov/about-us/cjis/ucr/crime-in-the-u.s/2012/crime-in-the-u.s.-2012/tables/1tabledatadecoverviewpdf/table_1_crime_in_the_united_states_by_volume_and_rate_per_100000_inhabitants_1993-2012.xls

Illinois report card, 2013-2014. (n.d.). Illinois State Board of Education. Retrieved from http://www.illinoisreportcard.com/School.spx?source=Trends&source2=GraduationRate&School-id=500821890220043

INROADS. (n.d.). Retrieved from http://www.inroads.org/inroads/inroadsHome.jsp

Kozol, J. (1991). *Savage inequalities: Children in America's schools.* New York: Crown.

Overmier, J., & Seligman, M. (1967). Effects of inescapable shock upon subsequent escape and avoidance responding. *Journal of Comparative and Physiological Psychology*, 63(1), 28-33.

Sylte, A. (2014, February 12). Baldwin ranked 9th safest city, East St. Louis most dangerous. Retrieved from http://www.ksdk.com/story/news/2014/02/12/ballwin-missouri-safest-city-ranking-east-st-louis-dangerous-neighborhood-scout/5432379/

Tatum, B. D. (2003). *Why are All the black kids sitting together in the cafeteria: And other conversations about race.* New York: Basic.

This is Ireland - Highlights from the 2011 census, part 1. (2011). Central Statistics Office. Retrieved from http://www.cso.ie/en/media/csoie/census/documents /census2011pdr/Census%202011%20Highlights%20Part%201%20web%2072dpi.pdf

Zinshteyn, M. (2015, February 17). The skills gap: America's young workers are lagging behind: New findings suggest that U.S. millennials are far less competent than their peers in Europe and Asia. *The Atlantic.*

Chapter 2

Associated Press (2014, July 22). Illegal immigration numbers: Border-crossing arrests near historic low. *San Jose Mercury News.* Retrieved from http://www.mercurynews.com/immigration/ci_26194454/illegal-immigration-border-crossing-arrests-near-historic-low

Associated Press. (2013, May 1). Cannibal colonists! Remains at Jamestown show early American settlers ate each other: scientists. *New York Daily News.* Retrieved from http://www.nydailynews.com/news/national/english-colonists-jamestown-cannibals-scientists-article-1.1332196

Bump, P. (2015, July 2). Surprise! Donald Trump is wrong about immigrants and crime. *The Washington Post.* Retrieved from http://www.washingtonpost.com/blogs/the-fix/wp/2015/07/02/surprise-donald-trump-is-wrong-about-immigrants-and-crime/

Brunner, B. & Rowen, B. (2007). Timeline of affirmative action milestones. *Infoplease.* Retrieved from http://www.infoplease.comspotaffirmativetimeline1.html#ixzz2vOnmouN

Camarota, S. A. & Vaughan, J. (2009). Immigration and crime: Assessing a conflicted issue. Center for Immigration Studies. Retrieved from http://cis.org/ImmigrantCrime

Churchill, W. (2004). *Kill the Indian, save the man.* San Francisco: City Lights Books.

Diner, H. R. (2004). *The Jews of the United States, 1654 to 2000.* Berkeley: University of California Press.

Dylan, B. (1963). Only a pawn in their game. *The times they are a-changin'.* Warner Brothers, Incorporated. Retrieved from http://www.bobdylan.com/us/songs/only-pawn-their-game#ixzz3aZxDQ9iL

Ehrenfreund, M. (2014, November 20). Your complete guide to

Obama's immigration executive action. *The Washington Post.* Retrieved from http://www.washingtonpost.com/blogs/wonkblog/wp/2014/11/19/your-complete-guide-to-obamas-immigration-order/#order

Hair, P. (2014, September 7). This football season, let's wipe 'Redskins' from our vocabulary. Retrieved from http://www.msnbc.com/msnbc/football-season-lets-wipe-redskins-our-vocabulary#

Hooper, K. & Batalova, J. (2015, January 28). Chinese Immigrants in the United States. Retrieved from http://www.migrationpolicy.org/article/chinese-immigrants-united-states

Hyman, P. E. (n.d.). Eastern European Immigrants in the United States. *Jewish Women's Archive Encyclopedia.* Retrieved from http://jwa.org/encyclopedia

Internment history. *WJCT.* Retrieved from http://www.pbs.org/childofcamp/history/

Karabel, J. (2006). *The chosen: The hidden history of admission and exclusion at Harvard, Yale, and Princeton.* New York. Houghton Mifflin Company.

Library of Congress. (n.d.). From haven to home: 350 years of Jewish life in America. Retrieved from http://www.loc.gov/exhibits/haventohome/haven-century.html

Library of Congress. (n.d.). Hawaii: Life in a plantation society. Retrieved from http://www.loc.gov/teachers/classroommaterials/presentationsandactivities/presentations/immigration/japanese2.html

Lopez, I. H. (1997). *White by law: The legal construction of race (critical America).* New York: New York University Press.

Peterson, L. (n.d.). Not just whistling Dixie in D.C.. Retrieved from http://espn.go.com/page2/wash/s/closer/020315.html

Sanders, S. H. (2014). Deaths at US-Mexico border reach 15-year low. *NPR.* Retrieved from http://www.npr.org/sections/thetwo-way/2014/10/23/358370958/deaths-at-us-mexico-border-reach-15-year-low

Takaki, R. (1993). *A different mirror: A history of multicultural America.* Boston: Back Bay Books.

United States Census Bureau. (2010). Race reporting for the Asian population by selected categories: 2010. Retrieved from http://factfinder.census.gov/faces/tableservices/jsf/pages/productview.xhtml?src=bkmk

United States Department of State, Office of the Historian (n.d.). Chinese Immigration and the Chinese Exclusion Acts. Retrieved from https://history.state.gov/milestones/1866-1898/chinese-immigration

United States policy toward Jewish refugees, 1941 - 1952. (2014, June 20). In *Holocaust Encyclopedia*. Retrieved from http://www.ushmm.org/wlc/en/article.php?ModuleId=10007094

Wei, W. (n.d.). The Chinese-American experience: An introduction. *Harp Week.* Retrieved from http://immigrants.harpweek.com/ChineseAmericans /1Introduction/BillWeiIntro.htm

Zirin, D. & Zill, Z. (2011, February 9). A history lesson for the Redskins owner: Dan Snyder needs a reminder about his team's attempts to resist integration. *The Nation.* Retrieved from http://www.thenation.com/article/158409/history-lesson-redskins-owner#

CHAPTER 3

African American chairman & CEO's of Fortune 500 companies. (2015, January 29). *Black Entrepreneur Profile.* Retrieved from http://www.blackentrepreneurprofile.com/fortune-500-ceos/

Background readings. (n.d.) In *Race: The power of an illusion.* Retrieved from http://www.pbs.org/race/000_About/002_04-background-03-02.htm

Bureau of Labor Statistics. (n.d.). Employment status of the civilian non-institutional population 25 years and over by educational attainment, sex, race, and Hispanic or Latino ethnicity. Retrieved from http://www.bls.gov/cps/cpsaat07.pdf

Bureau of Labor Statistics. (n.d.). Median weekly earnings by educational attainment in 2014. Retrieved from http://www.bls.gov/opub/ted/2015/median-weekly-earnings-by-education-gender-race-and-ethnicity-in-2014.htm

Bureau of Labor Statistics. (n.d.). Employment status of the civilian population by race, sex, and age. Retrieved from http://www.bls.gov/news.release/empsit.t02.htm

Brunner, B. & Rowen, B. (2007). Timeline of affirmative action milestones. *Infoplease.* Retrieved from http://www.infoplease.comspotaffirmativetimeline1.html#ixzz2vOnmouN 2

Centers for Disease Control and Prevention (CDC). (2013). *CDC Health Disparities & Inequalities Report.* Retrieved from http://www.cdc.gov/minorityhealth/CHDIReport.html#Intro

Denavas-Walt, C. & Proctor, B.D. (2014). Income and poverty in the United States: 2013. Retrieved from https://www.census.gov/content/dam/Census/library/publications/2014/demo/p60-249.pdf

Dewan, S. (2005, June 22). Ex-Klansman guilty of manslaughter in 1964 deaths. *New York Times.* Retrieved from http://query.nytimes.com/gst/fullpage.html?res=9F03EFD 9113BF931A-15755C0A9639C8B63&pagewanted=all

Dutko, P., Van Ploeg, M., & Farrigan, T. (2012). Characteristics and influential factors of food deserts. Retrieved from http://www.ers.usda.gov/media/883903/err140.pdf

Herbert, B. (2007, November 13). Righting Reagan's wrongs? *New York Times.* Retrieved from http://www.nytimes.com/2007/11/13/opinion/13herbert.html?_r=1&

Hirsch, J. S. (2002). *Riot and remembrance: The Tulsa race war and its legacy.* New York: Houghton Mifflin Company.

Gates, Jr., H. L. (2012, October 22). Who was the first African American? 100 amazing facts about the Negro: We know his name, and that he arrived well before the Mayflower. *The Root*. Retrieved from http://www.theroot.com/articles/history/2012/10/who_was_the_first_african_american_100_amazing_facts_about_the_negro.html

Iaccarino, A. (n. d.). The founding fathers and slavery. Retrieved from http://www.britannica.com/EBchecked/topic/1269536/The-Founding-Fathers-and-Slavery

Kena, G., Aud, S., Johnson, F., Wang, X., Zhang, J., Rathbun, A., Wilkinson-Flicker, S., and Kristapovich, P. (2014). The Condition of Education 2014.

Kochhar, R. & Fry, R. (2014, December 12). Wealth inequality has widened along racial, ethnic lines since end of Great Recession. *Pew Research Center*. http://www.pewresearch.org/fact-tank/2014/12/12/racial-wealth-gaps-great-recession/

Lawrence, K., Sutton, S., Kubisch, A., Susi, G. & Fulbright-Anderson, K. (2004). *Structural racism and community building*. Washington, D.C.: The Aspen Institute.

Leuchtenburg, W. E. (n.d.). Franklin D. Roosevelt: The American franchise. *University of Virginia Miller Center*. Retrieved from http://millercenter.org/president/biography/fdroosevelt-the-american-franchise

Lowrey, A. (2013). Wealth gap among races has widened since recession. *New York Times*. Retrieved from http://www.nytimes.com/2013/04/29/business/racial-wealth-gap-widened-during-recession.html?_r=0

Lynching in America: Confronting the legacy of racial terror. *Equal Justice Initiative*. Retrieved from http://www.eji.org/lynchinginamerica/

Moore, A. (2013, December 4). 8 successful and aspiring black communities destroyed by white neighbors. *Atlanta Black Star*. http://atlantablackstar.com/2013/12/04/8-successful-aspiring-black-communities-destroyed-white-neighbors/4/

National Archives. (n.d.). Americas founding fathers: Delegates to the constitutional convention. Retrieved from http://www.archives.gov/exhibits/charters/constitution_ founding_fathers.html

Painter, N. I. (2006). *Creating black Americans: African-American history and its meanings, 1619 to the present.* New York: Oxford University Press.

Perlstein, R. (n.d.). Exclusive: Lee Atwater's infamous 1981 interview on the southern strategy: The forty-two-minute recording, acquired by James Carter IV, confirms Atwater's incendiary remarks and places them in context. *The Nation.* Retrieved from http://www.thenation.com/article/170841/exclusive-lee-atwaters-infamous-1981-interview-southern-strategy

Race timeline - go deeper. (n.d.) In *Race: The power of an illusion.* Retrieved from http://www.pbs.org/race/000_About/002_04-background-02-12.htm

Ripley, W. (1899). *The races of Europe: A sociological study.* New York: D. Appleton and Company.

Roake, J. (2010, September 22). Think globally, act locally: Steve Lerner, 'Sacrifice Zones,' at politics and prose. *The Washington Post.* Retrieved from http://www.washingtonpost.com/express/wp/2010/09/23/steve-lerner-book-sacrifice-zones/

Rovner, J. (2014). Disproportionate minority contact in the juvenile jail system.

Retrieved from http://sentencingproject.org/doc/publications/jj_Disproportionate%20Minority%20Contact.pdf

The Sentencing Project. (2014). Facts about prisons and people in prison. Retrieved from http://sentencingproject.org/doc/publications/inc_Facts%20About%20Prisons.pdf

Takaki, R. (1993). *A different mirror: A history of multicultural America.* Boston: Back Bay Books.

United States Census Bureau. (2011). Census Bureau reports the number of black-owned businesses increased at triple the national rate. Retrieved from https://www.census.gov/newsroom/releases/archives/business_ownership/cb11-24.html

United States Department of Education, Office for Civil Rights Civil Rights (2014, March 21) Data collection: Data snapshot - teacher equity. Retrieved from http://www2.ed.gov/about/offices/list/ocr/docs/crdc-teacher-equity-snapshot.pdf

United States Department of Housing and Urban Development, Office of Policy Development and Research. (n.d.). Public Housing: Image Versus Facts. Retrieved from http://www.huduser.org/periodicals/ushmc/spring95/spring95.html

Wormser, R. (n.d.). Red summer (1919). *PBS*. Retrieved from http://www.pbs.org/wnet/jimcrow/stories_events_red.html

CHAPTER 4

Akers, M. D., & Porter, G. L. (2003). Your EQ skills: Got what it takes? *Journal of Accountancy*, 195(3), 65–69.

Asemota, A. O., George, B. P., Cumpsty-Fowler, C. J., Haider, A. H., & Schneider, E. B. (2013). Race and insurance disparities in discharge to rehabilitation for patients with traumatic brain injury. *Journal Neurotrauma*, 30(24), 2057 - 2065. Retrieved from http://www.ncbi.nlm.nih.gov/pubmed/23972035

Avenant, A., Sirigu, A., & Agliot, S. M. (2010). Racial bias reduces empathic sensorimotor resonance with other-race pain. *Current Biology*, 20(11),1018–1022. Retrieved from http://www.cell.com/current-biology/abstract/S0960-9822(10)00515-4

Bar-On, R. (1997). *The emotional quotient inventory: Technical manual.* Toronto: Multi-Health.

Bar-On, R., Tranel, D., Denburg, N. L., & Bechara, A. (2003). Exploring the neurological substrate of emotional and social intelligence. *Brain*, 126(8), 1790–1800.

Bar-On, R., & Parker, J. D. A. (2000). *The Bar-On Emotional Quotient Inventory: Youth Version (EQ-i:YV)* Technical Manual. Toronto, Canada: Multi-Health Systems, Inc.

Bavishi, A., Madera, J. M., & Hebl, M. R. (2010). The effect of professor ethnicity and gender on student evaluations: Judged before met. *Journal of Diversity in Higher Education*, 3(4), 245-256. Retrieved from http://psycnet.apa.org/index.cfm?fa=buy.optionToBuy&id=2010-22434-001

Binet, A., & Simon, T. (1916). *The development of intelligence in children*. Baltimore: Williams & Wilkins.

Berman, J. (2014, May 20). The job market discriminates against black college grads. *The Huffington Post*. Retrieved from http://www.huffingtonpost.com/2014/05/20/black-college-graduates_n_5358983.html?

Berman, T. (2008). Are you a good Samaritan? What would you do? Retrieved from http://abcnews.go.com/Primetime/WhatWouldYouDo/Story?id=4420829&page=3

Bertrand, M. & Mullainathan, S. (2004). Are Emily and Greg more employable than Lakisha and Jamal? A field experiment on labor market discrimination. *American Economic Review*, 94(4), 991-1013. Retrieved from https://ideas.repec.org/a/aea/aecrev/v94y-2004i4p991-1013.html

Bouie, J. (2014, July 24). The crisis in black home ownership: How the recession turned owners into renters and obliterated black American wealth. *Slate*. Retrieved from http://www.slate.com/articles/news_and_politics/politics/2014/07/black_homeownership_how_the_recession_turned_owners_into_renters_and_obliterated.2.html

Brewster, Z. & Lynn, M. (2014). Black–white earnings gap among restaurant servers: A replication, extension, and exploration of consumer racial discrimination in tipping. *Sociological Inquiry*, 84(4), 545–569. Retrieved from http://onlinelibrary.wiley.com/doi/10.1111/soin.12056/abstract

Bureau of Labor Statistics. (n.d.). Median weekly earnings by educational attainment in 2014. Retrieved from http://www.bls.gov/opub/ted/2015/median-weekly-earnings-by-education-gender-race-and-ethnicity-in-2014.htm

Carroll, J. B. (1997). Psychometrics, intelligence, and public perception. *Intelligence, 24,* 25–52.

Carson, B., & Lewis, G. (2000). *The big picture: Getting perspective on what is really important in life. Grand* Rapids, MI: Zondervan.

Caruso, D. R., Mayer, J. D., & Salovey, P. (2002). Relation of an ability measure of emotional intelligence to personality. *Journal Personality Assessment, 79*(2), 306–320.

Chabris, C. & Simons, D. (2011). *The invisible gorilla: How our intuitions deceive us.* New York: Crown. Chekroud, A. M., Everett, J. A. C., Bridge, H. & Hewstone, M. (2014). A review of neuroimaging studies of race-related prejudice: Does amygdala response reflect threat? *Frontiers in Human Neuroscience, 8,* 179. Retrieved from http://www.ncbi.nlm.nih.gov/pmc/articles/PMC3973920/

Chen, S. (2012, February 24). Lending discrimination: Black borrowers face higher hurdles, study shows. *Huffington Post.* Retrieved from http://www.huffingtonpost.com/2012/02/24/lending-discrimination-black-borrowers-face-higher-hurdles-in-lending-study_n_1300509.html

Conrad, J. (2006). The relationship between emotional intelligence and intercultural sensitivity (Doctoral dissertation). University of North Florida.

Cooper, R. K., & Sawaf, A. (1997). *Executive EQ: Emotional intelligence in leadership and organizations.* New York: Grosset/Putnam.

Cunningham W. A., Johnson M. K., Raye C. L., Gatenby J., Gore J. C., & Banaji M. R. (2004). Separable neural components in the processing of black and white faces. *Psychological Science, 15,* 806–813.

Damasio, A. R. (1994). *Descartes' error: Emotion, reason, and the human brain*. New York: Avon Books.

Duke Social Sciences Research Institute. (2014, February 27). Housing disparities: Are minorities paying more for housing? Retrieved from https://ssri.duke.edu/news/housing-disparities-are-minorities-paying-more-housing

Einstein, A. (1996). *Out of my later years*. New York: Wings Books.

Gardner, H. (1983). *Frames of mind: The theory of multiple intelligences*. New York: Basic Books.

Gardner, H. (1998). A multiplicity of intelligences. *Scientific American presents. Intelligence*, 9, 18–23.

Gardner, H. (2011). The theory of multiple intelligences: As psychology, as education, as social science. Retrieved from https://howardgardner01.files.wordpress.com/2012/06/473-madrid-oct-22-2011.pdf

Godette, D. C., Mulatu, M. S., Leonard, K.J., Randolph, S., & Williams, N. (2011). Racial/ethnic disparities in patterns and determinants of criminal justice involvement among youth in substance abuse treatment programs. *Journal of Correct Healthcare*, 17(4), 294 - 308. Retrieved from http://www.ncbi.nlm.nih.gov/pubmed/21821605

Goleman, D. (1995). *Emotional intelligence*. New York: Bantam Books.

Goleman, D. (1998). *Working with emotional intelligence*. New York: Bantam Books.

Goleman, D. (2005). *Emotional intelligence (10th anniversary ed.)*. New York: Bantam Books.

Goleman, D., Boyatzis, R. E., & McKee, A. (2002). *Primal leadership: Realizing the power of emotional intelligence*. Boston: Harvard Business School Press.

Gonzalez, G. (2013, June 11). Racial and economic minorities face more subtle housing discrimination: HUD study finds decline in blatant discrimination while unequal treatment persists. Retrieved from http://portal.hud.gov/hudportal/HUD?src=/press/ press_releases_media_advisories/2013/HUDNo.13-091

Hart A. J., Whalen P. J., Shin L. M., McInerney S. C., Fischer H., & Rauch S. L. (2000). Differential response in the human amygdala to racial outgroup vs ingroup face stimuli. *Neuroreport* 11, 2351–2355

Howard, P. J. (2006). *The owner's manual for the brain (Third ed.)*. Austin, TX: Bard.

Johnson, R., Roter, D., Powe, N. R., & Cooper, L. (2004). Patient race/ethnicity and quality of patient–physician communication during medical visits. American *Journal of Public Health*, 94(12), 2084-2090. Retrieved from http://www.ncbi.nlm.nih.gov/pmc/articles/PMC1448596/

Kaplan, R. M. & Saccuzzo, O. P. (2009). *Psychological testing: Principles, applications, and issues (7 ed.)*. Belmont, CA: Wadsworth).

Keith, T. Z. (1994). Intelligence is important, intelligence is complex. *School Psychology Quarterly*, 9, 209–221.

Kosslyn, S. M. & Miller, G. W. (2013). There is no left brain/right brain divide. *Time*. Retrieved from http://ideas.time.com/2013/11/29/there-is-no-left-brainright-brain-divide/

Krill A., Platek S. M. (2009). In-group and out-group membership mediates anterior cingulate activation to social exclusion. *Frontiers Evolutionary Neuroscience*, 1:1

LeDoux, J. E. (1996). *The emotional brain: The mysterious underpinnings of emotional life*. London, England: Simon & Schuster.

Mayer, J. D., Caruso, D. R., & Salovey, P. (1999). Emotional intelligence meets traditional standards for an intelligence. Retrieved from http://www.unh.edu/emotional_intelligence/EI%20Assets/Reprints...EI%20Proper/EI1999MayerCarusoSaloveyIntelligence.pdf

Mayer, J. D., Salovey, P., & Caruso, D. (2000). Models of emotional intelligence. In R. J. Sternberg (Ed.), *Handbook of Intelligence* (pp. 396–422). Cambridge, UK: University Press.

Mullainathan, S. (2015, January 3). Racial bias, even when we have good intentions. *New York Times.* Retrieved from http://www.ny-times.com/2015/01/04/upshot/the-measuring-sticks-of-racial-bias-.html?abt=0002&abg=1&_r=0

National Association for the Advancement of Colored People (NAACP). (n.d.). Criminal justice fact sheet. Retrieved from http://www.naacp.org/pages/criminal-justice-fact-sheet

Neubauer, P. B., & Neubauer, A. (1990). *Nature's thumbprint: The new genetics of personality.* Reading, MA: Addison-Wesley.

Pager, Devah (2008, August 9). Study: Black man and white felon – same chances for hire. *CNN.* Retrieved from http://ac360.blogs.cnn.com/2008/08/09/study-black-man-and-white-felon-same-chances-for-hire/?hpt=ac_mid

Pai, Y., & Adler, S. A. (2001). *Cultural Foundations of Education (3rd ed.).* Upper Saddle River, NJ: Prentice-Hall.

Payne, R. K. (2005). *A Framework for Understanding Poverty (4th ed.).* Highlands, TX: aha!Process, Inc.

Pessoa, L. & Adolphs, R. (2010, November). Emotion processing and the amygdala: From a 'low road' to 'many roads' of evaluating biological significance. *Nature Reviews Neuroscience, 11*(11), 773-783. Retrieved from http://www.ncbi.nlm.nih.gov/pmc/articles/PMC3025529/

Pew Research Center. (2012). The rise of Asian Americans. Retrieved from http://www.pewsocialtrends.org/2012/06/19/the-rise-of-asian-americans/

Reeves, A. N. (2014). Written in black and white: Exploring confirmation bias in racialized perceptions of writing skills. Retrieved from http://www.nextions.com/wp-content/files_mf/14151940752014040114WritteninBlackandWhiteYPS.pdf

Phelps E. A., O'Connor K. J., Cunningham W. A., Funayama E. S., Gatenby J. C., Gore J. C., et al. (2000). Performance on indirect measures of race evaluation predicts amygdala activation. *Journal of Cognitive Neuroscience.* 12, 729–738.

Ramachandran, V. S. (2011). *The tell-tale brain: A neuroscientist's quest for what makes us human.* New York: W.W. Norton & Company

Salovey, P., & Mayer, J. D. (1990). Emotional intelligence. *Imagination, Cognition, and Personality,* 9(3), 185–211.

Salovey, P., & Sluyter, D. J. (1997). *Emotional development and emotional intelligence: Educational implications.* New York: Basic Books.

Simmons, S., & Simmons, J. C. (1997). Measuring emotional intelligence: *The groundbreaking guide to applying the principles of emotional intelligence.* Arlington, TX: Summit.

Stein, S., & Book, H. (2000). *The EQ edge.* Toronto, ON: Multi-Health Systems.

Sternberg, R. J. (Ed.). (2000). *Handbook of Intelligence.* Cambridge, UK: University Press.

Stout, D. (2013, December 3). China is cheating the world student rankings system: Enough is enough: Beijing must supply national data to assessors and not simply the results of a small minority of elite students. *Time.* Retrieved from http://world.time.com /2013/12/04/china-is-cheating-the-world-student-rankings-system/

Tammet, D. (2006). *Born on a blue day.* Great Britain: Hodder & Stoughton.

Taylor, C., & Jaquez, N. D. (2008). Confronted with teen "vandals." What would you do? Retrieved from http://www.abcnews.go.com/Primetime/WhatWouldYouDo

Taylor, C., & Jaquez, N. D. (2008). Public displays of rage: What would you do? Retrieved from http://abcnews.go.com/Primetime/WhatWouldYouDo /Story?id=4076903&page=3

Thorndike, E.L. (1920). Intelligence and its use. *Harper's Magazine,* 140, 227-235.

Treffert, D. A. (n.d.). The autistic savant. Wisconsin Medical Society. Retrieved from https://www.wisconsinmedicalsociety.org/professional/savant-syndrome/resources /articles/the-autistic-savant/

True Colors Product Overview. (2008). Retrieved from http://www.corvision.com/productDetails.do?no=0000412

United States Department of Education. (2015, March 24). Expansive survey of America's public schools reveals troubling racial disparities: Lack of access to preschool, greater suspensions cited. Retrieved from http://www.ed.gov/news/press-releases/expansive-survey-americas-public-schools-reveals-troubling-racial-disparities

Wechsler, D. (1958). *The measurement and appraisal of adult intelligence (4th ed.).* Baltimore: Williams & Wilkins.

Wheeler M. E., Fiske S. T. (2005). Controlling racial prejudice: social-cognitive goals affect amygdala and stereotype activation. *Psychological Science,* 16, 56–63

Wright, W. (1998). *Born that way: Genes, behavior, personality.* New York: Knopf.

Xu, X., Zuo, X., Wang, X., & Han, S. (2009). Do you feel my pain? Racial group membership modulates empathic neural responses. *The Journal of Neuroscience,* 29(26), 8525-8529. Retrieved from http://www.jneurosci.org/content/29/26/8525.abstract

CHAPTER 5

American Institute of Stress. (2014). Stress is killing you. Retrieved from http://www.stress.org/stress-is-killing-you/

American Psychological Association (APA). (2012). Stress in America: Our health at risk. Retrieved from https://www.apa.org/news/press/releases/stress/2011/final-2011.pdf

American Psychiatric Association. (2000). *Diagnostic and Statistical Manual of Mental Disorder 4th Edn Text Revision.* Washington, DC: American Psychiatric Association

American Psychiatric Association. (2013). *Diagnostic and Statistical Manual of Mental Disorders 5th Edn.* Washington, DC: American Psychiatric Association.

Badge of Life. (n.d.). Police suicide myths. Retrieved from http://www.badgeoflife.com/currentmyths.php

Bentley, S. (2005). Short history of PTSD: From Thermopylae to hue soldiers have always had a disturbing reaction to war. *Vietnam Veterans of America: The Veteran.* Retrieved from http://www.vva.org/archive/TheVeteran/2005_03 /feature_HistoryPTSD.htm

Bergland, C. (2014, February 12). Chronic stress can damage brain structure and connectivity: Chronic stress and high levels of cortisol create long-lasting brain changes. *Psychology Today.* Retrieved from https://www.psychologytoday.com/blog/the-athletes-way/201402/chronic-stress-can-damage-brain-structure-and-connectivity

Berton, M. W., & Stabb, S. D. (1996). Exposure to violence and post-traumatic stress disorder in urban adolescents. Retrieved from http://findarticles.com/p/articles/mi_m2248/is_n122_v31/ai_18435728

Brown, D. W., Anda, R. F., Tiemeier, H., Felitti, V. J., Edwards, V. J., Croft, J. B., & Giles, W. H. (2009). Adverse childhood experiences and the risk of premature mortality. *American Journal of Preventative Medicine.* Retrieved from http://www.ncbi.nlm.nih.gov/pubmed/19840693

Darling, D. (2008). Researchers: Suicide seems linked to PTSD. Retrieved from http://www.redding.com/news/2008/feb/24/researchers-suicide-seems-linked-ptsd

DeGruy, J. (n.d.). Post traumatic slave syndrome. Retrieved from http://joydegruy.com/resources-2/post-traumatic-slave-syndrome/

Ex-kidnap girl "sorry for captor." (2007). Retrieved from http://news. bbc.co.uk/2/hi/europe/6955741.stm

Federal Bureau of Investigation (n.d.). Murder: race, ethnicity, and sex of victim by race, ethnicity, and sex of offender, 2013. Retrieved from http://www.fbi.gov/about-us/cjis/ucr/crime-in-the-u.s/2013/crime-in-the-u.s.-2013/offenses-known-to-law-enforcement/expanded-homicide expanded_homicide_data_table_6_ murder_race_and_sex_of_vicitm_by_race_and_sex_of_offender_2013.xls

Fetus to mom: You're stressing me out! (2005). Retrieved from http://www.webmd.com/baby/features/fetal-stress

Friedman, T. L. (2005). *The World Is Flat*. New York: Farrar, Straus, and Giroux.

Goldenberg, R., Cliver, S., Mulvihill, F., Hickey, C., Hoffman, H., Howard, J., Klerman, L., & Johnson, M. (1996). Medical, psychological, and behavioral risk factors do not explain the increased risk for low birth weight among Black women. *American Journal of Obstetrics and Gynecology*, 175, 1317–1324.

Gore, A. (2008). *The Assault on Reason: How the Politics of Blind Faith Subvert Wise Decision-making*. New York: Penguin Group.

Griffin, G., & Studzinski, A. (2010). Illinois childhood trauma coalition white paper: Child trauma as a lens for the public sector. Retrieved from http://www.law.uchicago.edu/files/file/ICTC%20White%20 Paper%20120110.pdf

Henry J. Kaiser Family Foundation. (n.d.). Poverty rate by race/ethnicity. Retrieved from http://kff.org/other/state-indicator/poverty-rate-by-raceethnicity/ Howard, P. J. (2006). *The owner's manual for the brain (3rd ed.)*. Austin, TX: Bard.

Hudenko, W. (2007). PTSD and suicide. Retrieved from http://www.ncptsd.va.gov/ncmain/ncdocs/fact_shts/fs_suicide.html

Human Rights Watch. (2003). United States: Mentally ill mistreated in prison: More mentally ill in prison than in hospitals. Retrieved from http://www.hrw.org/news/2003/10/21/united-states-mental-ly-ill-mistreated-prison Istanbul protocol manual on the effective investigation and documentation of torture and other cruel, inhuman or degrading treatment or punishment. (1999). Geneva: United Nations. Retrieved from http://www.ohchr.org/Documents/Publications/training8Rev1en.pdf

King, J., & Flenady, V. (2002). Antibiotics for preterm labour with intact membranes. The *Cochrane Database System*. Retrieved from http://www.ncbi.nlm.nih.gov/pubmed/12519538

Kozol, J. (1991). *Savage inequalities: Children in America's schools.* New York: Crown.

Lu, M. C., & Halfon, N. (2003). Racial and ethnic disparities in birth outcomes: A life-course perspective. *Maternal and Child Health Journal, 7*(1), 13–30.

MacDorman, M. F., & Matthews, T. J. (2013). Infant deaths - United States, 2005 – 2008. Retrieved from http://www.cdc.gov/mmwr/preview/mmwrhtml/su6203a29.htm

Matthews, T., MacDorman, M., & Menacker, F. (2002). *Infant Mortality Statistics from the 1999 Period Linked Birth/Infant Death Data Set.* Hyattsville, MD: National Center for Health Statistics.

McGuire, C., & Norton, C. (1989). *Perfect victim: The true story of "The girl in the box" by the D.A. that prosecuted her captor.* New York: Dell.

Namnyak, M., Tufton, N., Szekely, R., Toal, M., Worboys, S., & Sampson, E. L. (2008). "Stockholm syndrome": Psychiatric diagnosis or urban myth? *Acta Psychiatrica Scandinavica, 117*(1), 4–11.

National Alliance on Mental Illness. (2003, March 1). Mental illness facts and numbers. Retrieved from http://www.nami.org/factsheets/mentalillness_factsheet.pdf

National Child Trauma Stress Network. (n.d.). Types of Traumatic Stress. Retrieved from http://www.nctsn.org/trauma-types#q2

PTSD Foundation of America. (n.d.). PTSD (post traumatic stress disorder). Retrieved from http://ptsdusa.org/what-is-ptsd/

Ralli, T. (2005). Who's a looter? In storm's aftermath, pictures kick up a different kind of tempest. *New York Times.* Retrieved from http://www.nytimes.com/2005/09/05/business/whos-a-looter-in-storms-aftermath-pictures-kick-up-a-different-kind-of-tempest.html?_r=0

Reinberg, S. (2011). CDC: Half of Americans will suffer from mental health woes. *USA Today.* Retrieved from http://usatoday30.usatoday.com/news/health/medical/health/medical/mentalhealth/story/2011-09-05/CDC-Half-of-Americans-will-suffer-from-mental-health-woes/50250702/1

Reynolds, T. (2007). Media probes Shawn Hornbeck, Ben Ownby "Holding" by Mark Devlin. Retrieved from http://www.postchronicle.com/cgi-bin/artman/exec/view.cgi?archive=5&num=59411

Rosenberg, S. D., Mueser, K. T., Friedman, M. J., Gorman, P. G., Drake, R. E., Vidaver,

R. M., Torrey, W. C., & Jankowski, M. K. (2001). Developing effective treatments for posttraumatic disorder among people with severe mental illness. *Psychiatric Services,* 52(11), 1453–1461.

Rutsch, P. (2015, February 10). Guess how much of Uncle Sam's money goes to foreign aid. Guess again! Retrieved from http://www.npr.org/sections/goatsandsoda/2015/02/10/383875581/guess-how-much-of-uncle-sams-money-goes-to-foreign-aid-guess-again

Safe Horizon. (n.d.). Child abuse facts. Retrieved from http://www.safehorizon.org/page/child-abuse-facts-56.html

Savitz, D., & Pastore, L. (1999). Causes of prematurity. In M. McCormick & J. Siegel (Eds.), *Prenatal Care: Effectiveness and Implementation* (pp. 80–82). Cambridge, UK: Cambridge University Press.

Singh, G., & Yu, S. (1995). Infant mortality in the United States: Trends, differentials and projections, 1950 through 2010. *American Journal of Public Health,* 85, 957–964.

Southwick, S. M., & Charney, D. S. (2012). *Resilience: The science of mastering life's greatest challenges.* New York: Cambridge University Press.

United States Department of Health and Human Services. (1999). A report of the Surgeon General. Retrieved from http://profiles.nlm.nih.gov/NN/B/B/H/S

Williams, J. (2006). *Enough: The phony leaders, dead-end movements, and culture of failure that are undermining Black America—and what we can do about it.* New York: Crown.

CHAPTER 6

Akers, M. D., & Porter, G. L. (2003). Your EQ skills: Got what it takes? *Journal of Accountancy*, 195(3), 65–69.

Bill Clinton regrets 'three strikes' bill. (2015, July 16). *BBC News.* Retrieved from http://www.bbc.com/news/world-us-canada-33545971

Casner-Lotto, J., & Barrington, L. (2006). Are they really ready to work? Employers' perspectives on the basic knowledge and applied skills of new entrants to the 21st Century U.S. workforce. The Conference Board, Corporate Voices for Working Families, Partnership for 21st Century Skills, Society for Human Resource Management (SHRM).

El Sistema: Changing lives through music. (2008). Retrieved from http://www.cbsnews.com/stories/2008/04/11/60minutes/main4009335.shtml

Feldman, L., Schiraldi, & Ziedenberg, J. (2001). Too little too late: President Clinton's prison legacy. *Justice Policy Institute.* Retrieved from http://www.justicepolicy.org/research/2061

Gates, Jr., H. L. (2013, January 7). The truth behind 'forty acres and a mule.' The Root. Retrieved from http://www.theroot.com/articles/history/2013/01/40_acres_and_a_mule_promise_to_slaves_the_real_story.html

Granoff, G. (2005). Schools behind bars: Prison college programs unlock the keys to human potential. Retrieved from http://www.educationupdate.com/archives/2005/May/html/FEAT-BehindBars.html

Maximum security education. (2007). Retrieved from http://www.bard.edu/bpi/media/60minutes The murderer of Mr. Lincoln. (1865). *The Philadelphia Inquirer*. Retrieved from http://www.nytimes.com/1865/04/21/news/murderer-mr-lincoln-extraordinary-letter-john-wilkes-booth-proof-that-he.html?pagewanted=1

Pai, Y., & Adler, S. A. (2001). Cultural foundations of education (3rd ed.). Upper Saddle River, NJ: Merrill Prentice Hall.

Plummer, B. (2013, April 29). The government is spending way more on disaster relief than anybody thought. *The Washington Post*. Retrieved from http://www.washingtonpost.com/blogs/wonkblog/wp/2013/04/29/the-government-is-spending-way-more-on-disaster-relief-than-anybody-thought/

Southwick, S. M., & Charney, D. S. (2012). *Resilience: The science of mastering life's greatest challenges*. New York: Cambridge University Press.

The Stanford marshmallow study. (2008). Retrieved from http://www.edwardjones.com/cgi/getHTML.cgi?page=/GBR/resources/money_smart/building_blocks/ marshmallow.html.

What we do. (n.d.). *Bard Prison Initiative*. Retrieved from http://bpi.bard.edu/what-we-do/

Chapter 7

Asian cultures. (n.d.). Retrieved from http://www.mnsu.edu/emuseum/cultural/oldworld/asia.html

Bennett, M. J. (2000). High profile: Dr. Bennett revitalizes the model for intercultural sensitivity. *Cultural Diversity at Work*, 12(3).

Campbell, T. C., & Campbell II, T. M. (2004). *The China study: Startling implications for diet, weight loss, and long-term health.* Dallas: BenBella Books.

Centers for Disease Control and Prevention (CDC). (n.d.). Chronic Diseases: The leading causes of death and disability in the United States. Retrieved from http://www.cdc.gov/chronicdisease/overview/

Gandhi, A. (n.d.). Active and passive violence. Retrieved from http://www.innerself.com/Behavior_Modification/violence_12192.htm

Gladwell, M. (2000). *The tipping point: How little things can make a big difference.* New York: Black Bay Books.

Howard, P. J. (2006). *The owner's manual for the brain (3rd ed.).* Austin, TX: Bard.

Ogden, C. L., Carroll, M. D., Kit, B. K., & Flegal, K. M. (2012). Prevalence of childhood and adult obesity in the United States, 2011-2012. *Journal of the American Medical Association,* 311(8):806-14. Retrieved from http://www.ncbi.nlm.nih.gov/pubmed/24570244

Pai, Y., & Adler, S. A. (2001). *Cultural foundations of education (3rd ed.).* Upper Saddle

River, NJ: Merrill Prentice Hall. Researcher studies gangs by leading one (n.d.). Retrieved from http://www.npr.org/templates/story/story.php?storyId=18003654

Teenage boy from Bridgend found hanged in latest suspected suicide: A 17-year-old boy from Bridgend has been found hanged, police said. (2008, December 29). *The Telegraph.* Retrieved from http://www.telegraph.co.uk/news/uknews/4015147/Teenage-boy-from-Bridgend-found-hanged-in-latest-suspected-suicide.html

United States Census Bureau. (n.d.). People quick facts, 2013. Retrieved from http://quickfacts.census.gov/qfd/states/00000.html

Wine grape varieties. (n.d.). Retrieved from http://www.cellarnotes.net/key_grape_varieties.html

AFTERWORD

George, J. M. (2000). Emotion and leadership: The role of emotional intelligence. *Human Relations*, 53(8), 1027–1055.

Southwick, S. M., & Charney, D. S. (2012). *Resilience: The science of mastering life's greatest challenges*. New York: Cambridge University Press.

About the Author

As CEO and President of The Conrad Consulting Group, Dr. Jarik Conrad presents inspiring workshops and keynotes to thousands of non-profit executives, business professionals, and educators each year. He also provides executive coaching services to leaders seeking to improve upon their ability to understand and motivate others.

He has held significant Human Resources positions with several notable Fortune 500 companies, including Pillsbury (General Mills), Union Carbide (Dow), Citigroup and CSX where he led the Human Resources department for the Technology Division. He has also led the Human Resources Department of the City of Jacksonville, Florida.

Dr. Conrad is a committed lifelong learner, holding a bachelor's degree from the University of Illinois, two master's degrees from Cornell University, and a doctor of education degree from the University of North Florida. He is also a certified Senior Professional in Human Resources (SPHR), a Society for Human Resources Management Certified Senior Professional (SHRM-CSP), a certified intercultural sensitivity expert, and a certified emotional intelligence expert.

Dr. Conrad also holds a certification in Plant-Based Nutrition and is a certified personal trainer. He is also the CEO of Sprouted Bean Health Systems, which helps people take control of their diet, fitness, and overall health.